Grand Shetland Adventure Knits

Gudrun Johnston & Mary Jane Mucklestone

Grand Shetland Adventure Knits

SEARCH PRESS

This edition published in the UK in 2026 by
Search Press Limited
Wellwood, North Farm Road,
Tunbridge Wells, Kent TN2 3DR

1 2 3 4 5 6 7 8 9 10

The original edition was published by
Laine Publishing Oy in 2023.

Photography by Sini Kramer
Graphic design by Anne-Mari Ahonen

ISBN: 978-1-80092-450-5

Bookmarked Hub

Additional written instructions for the 'Lucky Lines Pullover' (page 54) and the 'Virdek Shawl' (page 178) are available to download free from the Bookmarked Hub. Search for this book by title or ISBN: the passworded files can be found under 'Book Extras'. Membership of the Bookmarked online community is free: www.bookmarkedhub.com

Publishers' notes

Metric measurements are used in this book; the imperial conversions are rounded to the nearest ¼in. Always use either metric or imperial measurements, not a combination of both.

The Publishers and author can accept no responsibility for any consequences arising from the information, advice or instructions given in this publication.

For errata, please visit our website (www.searchpress.com) or the Bookmarked Hub (www.bookmarkedhub.com).

GPSR information can be found at
www.searchpress.com
Printed in China, RRD042026.

Follow the authors on Instagram:
- @gudrunjohnston
- @mjmucklestone

and YouTube:
- @theshetlandtrader
- @maryjanemucklestone1421

CONTENTS

HELLO AND WELCOME!

We invite you to join us on a knitting journey in Shetland.

We feel incredibly fortunate to have spent so much time exploring, discovering and relaxing on these islands. And we've wanted to share our Shetland adventures with other knitters from the beginning.

In 2014, we brought our first intrepid knitters to Shetland. After settling them into the spectacular Burrastow House B&B, our home base on the west side of Shetland, we watched them forge a bond with all this special place has to offer: the sweeping landscapes, the people and their heritage, the natural beauty, varied wildlife, and the moments of quiet awe that are so much a part of life on the islands. After many such rewarding group trips, we wanted to further spread the joy.

This book celebrates our time in Shetland together, two friends who made the dream of these trips a reality for many. Our essays included here touch on some of the things we most enjoy doing, and spotlight a few of our favourite places to visit. It's not intended as an in-depth travel guide but rather an invitation that might lead to your own adventure.

Of course, deciding what knitwear to bring is part of preparing for every trip to Shetland! We have included patterns for our favourite, most versatile items to pack – multi-use garments designed for protection from the elements, for hiking, enjoying a day in town, or lounging by the stove after a day of exploring. All reflect our shared aesthetic as well as our own personal style.

So come along with us. Witness the landscape. Meet the people. Watch the seabirds soar through the vast sky, listening to their songs. Spot seals, otters, and, if really lucky, the occasional pod of orcas. And knit. Knit yourself a grand adventure!

Gudrun Johnston

MARY JANE MUCKLESTONE

ABBREVIATIONS

approx: approximately

BOR: beginning of the round

CC: contrast colour

CDD: slip 2 sts together kwise, k1, p2sso (2 sts dec; centred)

CO: cast on

dec: decrease/decreased/decreases/decreasing

DPNs: double-pointed needles

DS: double stitch (used in German Short Rows; see Techniques, page 14, for additional information)

GSR: German Short Rows

inc: increase/increased/increases/increasing

k: knit

k1tbl: knit 1 through the back loop

k2tog: knit 2 sts together (1 st dec)

k2tog tbl: knit 2 sts together through their back loops (1 st dec)

kfb: knit into the front and back of 1 st (1 st inc)

kwise: knitwise, as if to knit

LHN: left-hand needle

M1: make 1; make a backwards loop on the RHN (1 st inc)

M1B: make 1 below; insert RHN from front to back into the right leg of the st below the st on the LHN and knit, then knit the next st (1 st inc)

M1L: make 1 left; insert LHN from front to back under horizontal strand between needles and knit into the back of this loop (1 st inc; leans left)

M1R: make 1 right; insert LHN from back to front under horizontal strand between needles and knit into the front of this loop (1 st inc; leans right)

M2: with LHN, pick up the strand between needles from front to back and then knit into the back and then into the front of this loop (2 sts inc)

MC: main colour

p: purl

p&k: pick up and knit

p1tbl: purl 1 through the back loop

p2sso: pass 2 slipped sts over the previously worked st

psso: pass slipped st over

PM: place marker

pwise: purlwise, as if to purl

rem: remain/remaining

rep: repeat(s)/repeating

RHN: right-hand needle

RM: remove marker

rnd(s): round(s)

RS: right side of fabric

sk2po: slip 1 st kwise, k2tog, psso

sl, sl1: slip/slip 1 st pwise unless otherwise indicated

sl2kw: slip 2 sts together kwise

SM: slip marker

ssk: slip 2 sts together kwise 1 at a time, return sts to LHN, k2tog tbl (1 st dec)

ssk (modified): slip 1 st kwise, return st to LHN, k2tog through back loops (1 st dec)

st(s): stitch(es)

st st: stocking (stockinette) stitch

tbl: through the back loops

W+T: wrap and turn (see Techniques, Short Row Wrap + Turn for additional information)

WS: wrong side of fabric

wyib: with yarn in back

wyif: with yarn in front

YO: yarn over

TECHNIQUES

AFTERTHOUGHT HEELS & THUMBS

Afterthought heels and thumbs are created by working a length of waste yarn into the fabric where the future heel or thumb will go, then slipping the stitches worked on waste yarn back to the left needle to be worked with the working yarn(s). This keeps the stitch patterns continuous throughout the piece. Despite the name, afterthought heels and thumbs worked from waste yarn stitches do require a bit of forethought to be placed at the appropriate site in the fabric; working the stitches later is the 'afterthought'. True afterthought heels and thumbs, created without the use of waste yarn, do exist but are not in the patterns presented in this book.

When ready to work the heel or thumb, return to the waste yarn and place the right leg of the stitches above and below the waste yarn on separate needle(s). Pay attention to whether the pattern instructs to pick up extra stitches at either end of the held stitches or not (if included, note whether these stitches are to be worked as is or if they are decreased on the following round). Once all stitches are securely picked up, gently tease out one end of the waste yarn and then continue to unweave it from the fabric. All live stitches are now on the needle(s) ready to be worked as instructed.

BACKWARDS LOOP CAST-ON

Step 1: Hold the needle to receive cast on stitches in your right hand with needle tip pointing to the left. Hold the working yarn over your left thumb so that the yarn end attached to the work is behind your thumb and the yarn end attached to the ball (the tail) is in front of your thumb. Grasp the tail end of the yarn with the fingers of your left hand.
Step 2: Bring your right needle tip towards you, so that the yarn attached to the work crosses over the tail.
Step 3: Bring the right needle tip up, parallel with your thumb, into the backwards loop of yarn that has formed on your thumb.
Step 4: Drop the loop off your thumb and onto the needle tip, tightening the loop on the needle.
Repeat steps 1–4 until all stitches are cast on.

BLOCKING

The following are general instructions for wet- and steam-blocking knitted fabric. Consult the yarn label of the particular yarn you are working with in regards to specific blocking recommendations made by your yarn's manufacturer. Refer to individual patterns for additional instructions specific to the item.

Wet-blocking
Soak item in a basin of cold or lukewarm water with a gentle wool wash (optional). With item fully submerged, leave item to soak for a minimum of 20 minutes. Then, if necessary, rinse to remove wool wash. Drain the basin and gently press on the item to remove additional water. Gently scoop up the item and spread it atop a clean towel without stretching the piece. Roll up the towel to remove additional excess water.

Lay the item out on top of a dry towel or blocking mats and block to finished measurements (for garments, see size tables). Hats may be blocked flat, atop a hat form or balloon, or stuffed with plastic bags. Leave item to dry before removing.

Steam-blocking
Items may be steam-blocked using either an iron or a hand-held steamer. If using an iron, never place a hot iron directly onto the knitted fabric; instead, hold it above the piece, preferably with a pressing cloth between the piece and the iron (use a dry pressing cloth if using a steam iron; use a wet pressing cloth if using a dry iron). Proceed as for wet-blocking.

CROCHET PROVISIONAL CAST-ON

With waste yarn in a contrasting colour and similar weight to your working yarn, create a slip knot and place the loop on the hook end of a crochet hook. Holding the crochet hook in your right hand and a knitting needle in your left hand, with needle on top of the working end of the waste yarn, *reach across the top of the needle with the crochet hook, grab the waste yarn, and pull the yarn through the loop on the crochet hook, creating a new loop on the crochet hook as well as a provisional stitch on the needle. Bring the waste yarn under and behind the knitting needle, then continue from * until all provisional stitches are cast on onto the needle.

To finish, chain a few additional loops using only the yarn and the crochet hook (omitting the knitting needle), break the waste yarn and pull the tail through the remaining loop. When ready to remove the waste yarn, begin at the end with extra chained loops; it will be easier to pull out the waste yarn from this end.

GERMAN SHORT ROWS

Note: When counting stitches in German Short Rows, count the DS (double stitch) as one stitch.

Working German Short Rows
Work to the turning point, turn the work, then make a DS (double stitch) as follows: slip 1 stitch (the last worked stitch) pwise wyif from LHN to RHN, then pulling the working yarn taut, take it up and over the RHN to the back of work (the slipped stitch will look like it has two legs, hence its name 'double stitch'). Keep tension/gauge on the DS as you work the next stitch (leaving yarn at back to knit or bringing yarn forwards to purl).

Resolving (Closing) German Short Rows When Working Flat
When you come to the gap created by the DS on the next row, close the two legs of the DS by working either k2tog or p2tog, depending on whether the stitch is to be a knit stitch or a purl stitch.

Resolving (Closing) German Short Rows When Working in the Round
For DSs created on the RS: Work to the DS, knit the two legs of the stitch together as one.

For DSs created on the WS (technique attributed to Patty Lyons): Work to 1 stitch before the DS and slip stitch kwise. Knit the first leg of the DS through the back loop. Pass the slipped stitch over. Knit the second leg of the DS through the back loop.

GERMAN TWISTED CAST-ON (AKA OLD NORWEGIAN CAST-ON)

The German Twisted Cast-On is similar to the Long-Tail Cast-On, with one additional twist. Follow the set-up for the Long-Tail Cast-On (including beginning with a long yarn tail), then proceed as follows:
Step 1: Bring needle under both strands that are around the thumb.
Step 2: Bring needle down through the loop formed by the thumb, then swivel thumb to untwist the thumb loop.
Step 3: Take the needle tip over the top of the front strand on the index finger to catch it.
Step 4: Bring the needle back down through the centre of the loop on the thumb.
Step 5: Remove thumb from its loop and tighten the stitch just formed on the RHN.
Step 6: Reposition yarn over thumb and index finger.
Repeat steps 1–6 until all stitches are cast on.

GRAFTING

Set-up: confirm that the stitches to be grafted are evenly divided between two needles. Hold the two needles parallel (with one in front and one in back) with both needles pointing to the right. Thread a length of sturdy seaming yarn (approx. three times the length of the graft) onto a tapestry needle.
Step 1: Bring the tapestry needle through the first stitch on the front needle pwise; leave stitch on the needle.
Step 2: Bring the tapestry needle through the first stitch on the back needle kwise; leave stitch on the needle.
Step 3: Bring tapestry needle through the first stitch on the front needle kwise and take it off the needle, then go into the next stitch on the front needle pwise; leave stitch on the needle.
Step 4: Bring tapestry needle through the first stitch on the back needle pwise and take it off the needle, then go into the next stitch on the back needle kwise; leave stitch on the needle.

Repeat steps 3 and 4 until all stitches have been grafted, checking your tension/gauge as you go (alternatively, work the graft loosely and then tighten up the graft to match the tension/gauge of the surrounding stitches once graft is complete).

I-CORD CAST- (BIND-) OFF

Cast on 3 stitches using Backwards Loop Cast-On, *k2, ssk, slip 3 stitches from RHN back to LHN; rep from * until you have 3 stitches remaining on LHN, sk2po, cut yarn leaving a tail and draw through remaining stitch.

LONG-TAIL CAST-ON

To work this cast on, you will need a long tail of yarn. One way to approximate this length is to wrap the yarn around the needle 10 times, to approximate 10 stitches, then multiply that length of yarn by the total stitch count divided by 10.
Set-up: once you have your yarn tail, make a slip knot and place the loop onto the RHN; this counts as your first stitch. Insert your left thumb and index finger in between the yarns hanging from the RHN, with the working yarn over your index finger and the tail over your thumb. Turn your left palm to face you, making a 'V' shape with the yarn. Close the other fingers of your left hand over the hanging ends of the yarn to keep the yarn in place.

Step 1: Bring the needle tip under the front strand on the thumb.
Step 2: Take the needle tip over the top of the front strand on the index finger to catch it.
Step 3: Bring the needle back down through the centre of the loop on the thumb.
Step 4: Remove thumb from its loop and tighten the stitch just formed on the RHN.
Step 5: Reposition yarn over thumb and index finger. Repeat steps 1–5 until all stitches are cast on.

MATTRESS STITCH FOR GARTER STITCH

On a flat surface, place the pieces to be seamed side-by-side with RSs facing up. Thread the tail or a new length of sturdy seaming yarn (in the same colour as the pieces to be seamed and approx. three times the length of the seam) onto a tapestry needle.

Beginning at the lower edge and working upward, *pull the needle through the bottom loop of the edge-most stitch on one piece, then pull the needle through the top loop of the edge-most stitch of the corresponding stitch on the other piece. Repeat from * until both pieces have been joined together. Adjust seaming tension/gauge as you go, aiming for a tension/gauge that is neither too tight nor too loose. (Alternatively, seam loosely then every 5cm/2in or so, gently pull upwards on the seaming yarn, allowing the two pieces to 'zip' together.)

STEEKS

Used in circular knitting where an opening is needed, steeks are extra stitches used to bridge the gap where the indended opening will sit, allowing you to continue knitting in the round. Later these extra stitches are cut down the middle, creating an opening for an armhole, or a neckline.

When you reach the point in your knitting where an opening is to begin, some of the working stitches are either cast (bound) off or placed on a holder. Steek stitches are then cast on above and the work is resumed. The number of steek stitches usually ranges between five and eight, utilizing both the pattern colour and the background colour, typically alternating every stitch. This makes a dense fabric with very short floats. Keeping the centre two stitches in the same colour makes it clear to see where to cut.

If you are using a traditional yarn like Shetland wool, it is possible to cut the steek open without any special finishing at all. Stitches are reluctant to unravel laterally and the 'grippy' nature of the wool keeps it in place. If you are fearful of the yarn unravelling, or are using a less forgiving yarn, try any of the following finishing methods, perhaps practising on a swatch first.

1. Machine-stitched Steek
The machine-stitched method is fast and easy for those comfortable using a sewing machine. The method is especially useful for large-diameter yarns, which may not stick together as readily as finer yarns do, and for slippery yarns such as superwash or alpaca. Machine stitching ensures that the yarns are locked into place.

Step 1: Using a sewing machine, sew a line of stitches down the centre of the stitches either side of the two centre stitches. Work a second line of machine stitching one stitch over from the first line of machine stitching.
Step 2: Carefully cut down the centre of the steek between the two centre stitches.

2. Handstitched Steek

Not everyone has a sewing machine; fortunately, careful hand sewing is just as effective as machine sewing and follows essentially the same process. I use ordinary sewing thread.
Step 1: Using a backstitch, sew a line of stitches down the centre of the stitches either side of the two centre stitches. Make another line of stitching down the centre of the next line of stitches.
Step 2: Carefully cut down the centre of the steek between the two centre stitches.

3. Crocheted Steek

Although a bit time-consuming, the crocheted steek creates a nice finished edge. I recommend using a crochet hook slightly smaller in diameter than the knitting needles you used. I also either use a yarn from my garment, choosing one I think is pretty, or find a similar but slightly finer yarn. A 2-ply jumper weight Shetland wool is ideal for using with the Peerie Shop Cardigan.

Begin by turning your work so that the left side of the opening is nearest you. You will be working a line of chain stitch crochet by connecting the outside half of one of the two centre steek stitches to the neighbouring half of the stitch next to it.

Step 1: Make a slip knot with the working yarn and place it on your hook.
Step 2: Pick up the loops of the closest centre stitch (the one at the bottom of the steek) and the one immediately below it with your hook.
Step 3: Wrap the yarn around the hook, then pull the hook through the two loops and the slip knot.
Step 4: Continue, picking up the next pair of stitches along the steek and pulling the working yarn through them and through the loop on the hook. When you reach the top of the steek, cut the yarn and pull it through the final loop.
Step 5: Turn the work 180° so that the righthand side of the steek is nearest you. Repeat steps 1–4 until you reach the end of the steek, then fasten off.
Step 6: Carefully cut down the centre of the steek between the two centre stitches. The cut edges will naturally roll to the wrong side along the crocheted stitches for a tidy finish.

THREE-NEEDLE CAST (BIND) OFF

Note: refer to individual patterns regarding set-up and whether to hold RS or WS together when working the cast (bind) off. This cast (bind) off requires the same number of stitches on each needle before beginning.

With stitches for pieces to be joined on needles (see pattern) and holding needles parallel to each other with tips pointing to the right, use a third needle to knit together one stitch from the front needle and one stitch from the back needle, *knit together one stitch from the front needle and one stitch from the back needle, cast (bind) off one stitch; repeat from * until all stitches are knit together and bound off. Break yarn leaving a tail and pull through remaining stitch.

WRAP + TURN SHORT ROWS

Worked over garter stitch
Note: it is not necessary to resolve wrapped stitches when working Wrap + Turn Short Rows in garter stitch as the wraps hide within the garter fabric.

(RS & WS): Work to the turning point, slip the next stitch pwise to the RHN, bring the yarn between the needles, return slipped stitch pwise to the LHN, turn work; yarn remains at back, ready to knit the next row. After working the next stitch, pull on the working yarn to tighten up the wrap.

YARN OVER AT BEGINNING OF A ROW

Hold the working yarn over the RHN as you work the first stitch on the LHN. Note that the working yarn simply sits over the RHN; do not wrap it around the RHN. Made at the beginning of rows, loose loops will form along the outside edges of the work.

Find helpful video tutorials on Gudrun and Mary Jane's individual YouTube channels (see page 6) as well as at maryjanemucklestone.com

WELCOME
TO
SHETLAND
MED
LÖGUM SKAL
LAND
BYGGJA

Olna Firth
Busta Voe
Swarbacks Minn
PAPA LITTLE
Aith Voe
West Kame
Mid Kame
Valley of Kergord
Petta Dale
East Kame
NORTH NESTING
Muckle Moor
Yelts Moor
Voe
Hillside
Grobsness
Lunga Water
Cole Deep
Olas Voe
Mangaster Voe
Mavis Grind
Brae
Busta
Wethersta
Hulness
Aith

A SHETLAND WELCOME

by Gudrun Johnston

However you arrive in Shetland, you are in for quite an experience. Taking the overnight ferry from Aberdeen gives you a real sense of just how remote these islands are. If you're up early you may even catch a glimpse of Fair Isle, situated 40km (25mi) from the southern end of Shetland. At the very least, be on deck for arrival into Lerwick Harbour and take a big, long gulp of the fresh, salty air waiting to welcome you.

Although I have enjoyed many boat trips, I frequently choose to come on the little plane instead (the North Sea can be rough)! Each time I fly in, my excitement mounts and my heart soars when the clouds break and I spot the Sumburgh Head Lighthouse and the tiny airstrip where the pilot will masterfully land the plane.

Our group trips usually involve people arriving by both modes of transport. As a result, our adventures often begin with collecting the intrepid ferry folk from Lerwick and then heading to the very southern tip of mainland Shetland where the flights arrive.

Once all are gathered, the first group activity happens moments from the airport. We take the single-track road to Sumburgh Head for some puffin spotting! Don't underestimate how captivating it is to watch these funny little birds waddle outside their burrows, nosily checking on the neighbours or battling the wind for takeoff – sometimes only to be blown straight back! It's like being in an actual nature documentary and it is the perfect way to start your Shetland experience.

Just down from Sumburgh Head is Jarlshof, an archaeological site steeped in over 4,000 years of human settlement all under one roof (or rather, layers of ruin). And – if we want to stretch our legs – we can walk there from our puffin-watching location along a coastal path. Just beware that if you are doing this in the summer months, you'll need to watch out for the Tirricks (terns) that may be nesting at the shore's edge. You can't miss their angry, protective shrieks and dive-bombing antics. If sighted, it's advisable to walk near a tall friend!

There are a lot of great beaches on the south mainland (and we pass a couple of them by the airport already) but one not to be missed is St Ninian's Isle. This spit of sand connects the mainland to the isle and is one of the UK's largest active tombolos. That means you have the sea on both sides and can explore two beaches in one! In the summer months, it is always accessible but at other times of the year, you may find the tombolo covered at high tide.

Of course, we like to make sure we also include some woolly-related visits on our first day. We are fortunate to have the opportunity to show two very different ends of the spectrum when it comes to the heritage and influence of knitwear in Shetland.

No trip here is complete without spending time at Nielanell, the studio of contemporary knitwear designer Niela Nell Kalra, in Hoswick. After a career as a criminal defence lawyer in Scotland, Niela found herself moving to Shetland in 2004 after visiting and then completing the textile degree programme at the college in Lerwick. Niela weaves in elements of her multicultural experience as a child of an Indian father and Scottish mother and draws on the influences surrounding her in Shetland, to inform her process. She always captivates our groups, warmly encouraging everyone to try things on and think about how the item makes them feel. Hopefully, you get to meet Niela herself as nothing compares to hearing her tell her story in her own words. It makes owning one of these unique items that much more special.

Continuing north we reach Cunninsburgh, home to Shetland-born designer Wilma Malcolmson. Stepping into Wilma's studio is a feast for the eyes for traditional knitwear lovers. Her exquisite talent for colour blending in Fair Isle knitting is evident in the swatches adorning the walls. Her story has been firmly imprinted in these islands for generations and continues to live on in her granddaughter, Terri Leask, who has followed in her footsteps establishing herself in a new lineage of knitwear designers in Shetland. Wilma and Terri often work together and welcome visiting knitters into the studio space for workshops and conversation. Wilma has beautiful, finished knitwear for sale and most people can't leave empty-handed.

Nature, history and woolly purchases satisfied for the day, we head to our idyllic surroundings at Burrastow House where more wonderful surprises await.

CAKE FRIDGE HAT

by Gudrun Johnston

Yes it's true – there is an actual fridge at the side of a road where one can purchase cakes and sweets. We always make sure that every person visiting Shetland gets to experience this phenomenon. The motifs and colours in this hat reminded me of having some fancy cake and tea, something Shetlanders love to do!

CONSTRUCTION

This hat is worked from the brim to the crown, beginning with a ribbed brim. Fair Isle charts are then worked for the body of the hat through the crown decreases. An optional pom-pom can be added.

SIZE

One size

FINISHED MEASUREMENTS

Circumference at brim: 45.5cm (18in)
Circumference at widest point: 54cm (21½in)
Length from brim to crown as worn: 23cm (9in)

Fits head circumferences 48–53cm (19–21in) with 2.5–7.5cm (1–3in) of negative ease.

MATERIALS

Yarn: 4-ply (fingering) weight yarn in the following approx. amounts:
MC: 105m (115yds)
CC1: 25m (30yds)
CC2: 10m (15yds)
CC3: 25m (30yds)
CC4: 10m (15yds)
CC5: 10m (15yds)
Approx. an additional 35m (40yds) total in chosen colour(s) for optional pom-pom.

Shown in: Jamieson's of Shetland Spindrift (100% pure Shetland wool, 25g/1oz/105m/115yds) in shades 246 Wren (MC), 122 Granite (CC1), 126 Charcoal (CC2), 766 Sage (CC3), 290 Oyster (CC4) and 301 Salmon (CC5)
MC, CC1, CC2, CC3, CC4 and CC5: 1 ball each

Needles:
Ribbing: 2.75mm (UK 12, US 2) set of DPNs or 40cm (16in) circular needle*
Main: 3.5mm (UK 10/9, US 4) set of DPNs or 40cm (16in) circular needle*
**For small circumference in the round; alternatively, use a long circular with the Magic Loop method.*

Always use needle size(s) needed to achieve tension/gauge.

Notions: 1 stitch marker, tapestry needle, pom-pom maker (optional)

TENSION/GAUGE

27 sts and 32 rounds = 10cm (4in) over Fair Isle Pattern worked in the round using main needle, after blocking

28 sts and 40 rounds = 10cm (4in) over Rib Pattern worked in the round using ribbing needle, after blocking

PATTERN NOTES

The colourwork charts include a guide for which is the pattern colour and which is the background colour when two colours are worked per round. Regardless of how you hold your yarn, hold the pattern colour to the left of the background colour; the float of the pattern colour should lie below the float of the background colour on the WS.

See Techniques for additional instructions on the German Twisted Cast-On and the Long-Tail Cast-On.

INSTRUCTIONS

BRIM

Using ribbing needle(s) and MC, CO 126 sts as follows (alternatively, use your favourite stretchy cast-on):
Make a slip knot and place on needle as the first st, CO 1 st using the German Twisted Cast-On, *CO 1 st using the Long-Tail Cast-On, then CO 1 st using the German Twisted Cast-On; rep from * until all sts are cast on.

PM for BOR and join for working in the round, being careful not to twist.

Rib Round: *k1, p1; rep from * to end of rnd.
Work rib round a total of 13 times or until ribbing measures 3.25cm (1¼in) from cast-on edge.

Inc Round: *work in rib pattern for 7 sts, M1L; rep from * to end of rnd (18 sts inc; 144 sts).

Change to main needle(s) and knit 1 rnd with MC.

COLOURWORK

Begin working from charts as follows, changing shades as indicated (see Pattern Notes above):
Next Round: Work across 6 sts from round 1 of Chart A to end of rnd.
Last rnd sets Chart A pattern. Continue to work from Chart A until rounds 1–11 have been worked.

Next Round: Work across 4 sts from round 1 of Chart B to end of rnd.
Last rnd sets Chart B pattern. Continue to work from Chart B until rounds 1–17 have been worked.

Next Round: Work across 6 sts from round 1 of Chart A to end of rnd.
Last rnd sets Chart A pattern. Continue to work from Chart A until rounds 1–11 have been worked.

SHAPE CROWN

Note: During the crown shaping, 12 sts are decreased every Dec Round (see chart). Before working each Dec Round, stop 1 st before the beginning of previous rnd, sl1 pwise, remove BOR marker, return slipped st to LHN pwise, replace BOR marker; work Dec Round as instructed by chart.

Next Round: work across 24 sts from round 1 of Chart C to end of rnd.
Last rnd sets Chart C pattern. Continue to work from Chart C, changing yarns and decreasing as indicated (see note above), until Chart C is complete (132 sts dec; 12 sts).

FINISHING

Break yarns. Pull MC yarn tail through rem sts, then secure tails to the inside of the hat. Weave in ends on the WS.

Soak hat in lukewarm water and a gentle wool wash (optional) for 20–30 minutes. Remove excess water by carefully squeezing (not wringing) and then press hat between towels. Lay hat flat, place on a hat form, or stuff with plastic bags and leave to dry. Make and attach pom-pom (optional).

CHART A

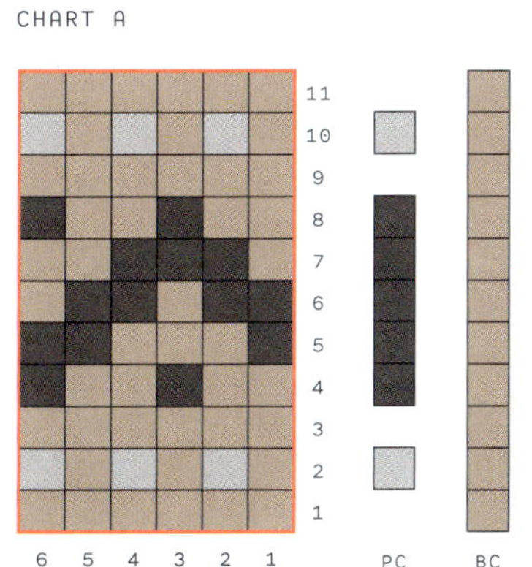

CHART B

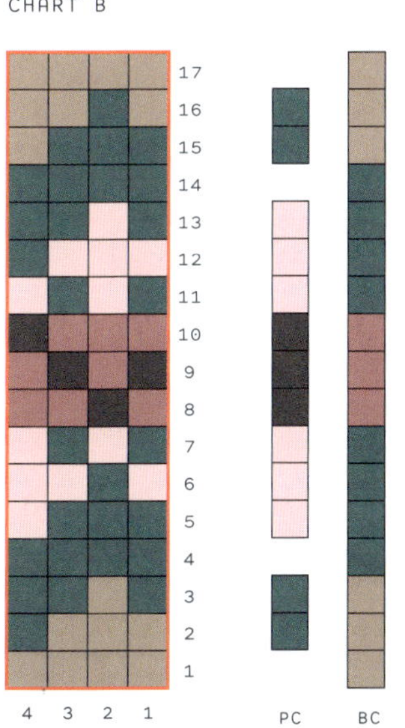

CHART C

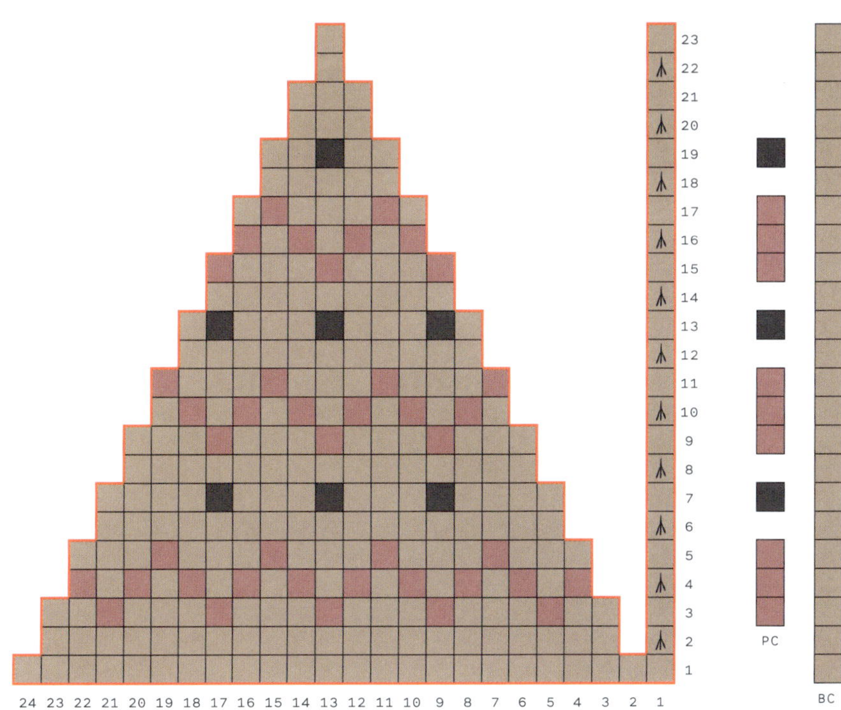

STANEYDALE SCARF

by Mary Jane Mucklestone

Lace knitting in Shetland is a high art and I'm an absolute novice. This scarf is as simple as it gets, with a stacked flower motif inspired by the Unst Eyelid lace pattern alternating with strips of ribbing. It reminds me of long narrow fields, some cultivated and blooming and others ploughed but left fallow.

CONSTRUCTION

This rectangular lace scarf is worked flat, featuring a lace pattern on a garter stitch background. Ribbed borders and edges complete the scarf. The lace pattern is both charted and written.

SIZE

One size

FINISHED MEASUREMENTS

Width: 25cm (10in)
Length: 157.5cm (62in)

MATERIALS

Yarn: approx. 455m (500yds) of 4-ply (fingering) weight yarn

Shown in: Biches & Bûches Le Petit Lambswool (100% lambswool; 50g/1¾oz/248m/270yds) in shade Dark Orange Grey
2 balls

Needles: 3.25mm (UK 10, US 3) circular needle, 40cm (16in) length

Notions: 2 stitch markers, tapestry needle, blocking wires and/or T-pins (optional)

TENSION/GAUGE

Exact tension/gauge is not critical but will affect overall scarf dimensions.

24 sts and 27 rows = 10cm (4in) over Ribbing and Eyelid Pattern worked flat, after blocking

PATTERN NOTES

Both written and charted instructions are provided for the rib and lace patterns.

Yarn overs are worked as double YOs on the RS; work them as one stitch on the WS.

INSTRUCTIONS

CAST ON

CO 61 sts using your favourite stretchy cast-on.

Set-up Row 1 (RS): k1, *k1, p1; rep from * to last 2 sts, k2.
Set-up Row 2 (WS): sl1 wyif, *p1, k1; rep from * to end of row.

BORDER

Row 1 (RS): sl1 wyif, *k1, p1; rep from * to last 2 sts, k2.
Row 2 (WS): sl1 wyif, *p1, k1; rep from * to end of row.
Repeat rows 1 and 2 in Border rib pattern until piece measures 5cm (2in), ending on a WS row.

BODY

Note: stitch markers are placed on the first Set-Up Row to mark where the edging meets the Chart pattern.

Set-up Row 1 (RS): sl1 wyif, (k1, p1) four times, k1, PM, work row 1 of Eyelid Lace from either the chart or written instructions, PM, (k1, p1) four times, k2.
Row 2 (WS): sl1 wyif, (p1, k1) four times, p1, SM, work next row of Eyelid Lace from either the chart or written instructions, SM, (p1, k1) to end of row.

Work in established pattern until piece measures approx. 152.5cm (60in) from CO edge or 5cm (2in) less than desired total length, ending with row 14 of chart. Work row 1 of the Chart one more time.

END BORDER

Row 1 (WS): sl1 wyif, *p1, k1; rep from * to end of row.
Row 2 (RS): sl1 wyif, *k1, p1; rep from * to last 2 sts, k2.
Repeat rows 1 and 2 in End Border rib pattern until piece measures 5cm (2in), ending on a RS row.

Cast (bind) off all sts loosely in rib pattern.

FINISHING

Weave in ends.

Wet block or steam block to finished measurements.

For best results, block scarf using blocking wires, threading wires through the slipped sts on the sides of the scarf. For the top and bottom, you can use either blocking wires or T-pins along the cast-on and cast- (bound-) off edges.

EYELID LACE CHART WRITTEN INSTRUCTIONS

Note: yarn overs are worked as double YOs on the RS; work them as one stitch on the WS.

Row 1 (RS): *k10, (p1, k1) three times; rep from * to last 9 sts, k9.
Row 2 and all WS rows: k9, *(p1, k1) three times, p1, k9; rep from * to end of row.
Row 3: rep row 1.
Row 5: *k2, k2tog, (YO) twice, k1, (YO) twice, ssk, k3, (p1, k1) three times; rep from * to last 9 sts, k2, k2tog, (YO) twice, k1, (YO) twice, ssk, k2.
Row 7: *k1, k2tog, (YO) twice, k3, (YO) twice, ssk, k2, (p1, k1) three times; rep from * to last 9 sts, k1, k2tog, (YO) twice, k3, (YO) twice, ssk, k1.
Row 9: *k2, (YO) twice, ssk, (YO) twice, CDD, (YO) twice, k3, (p1, k1) three times; rep from * to last 9 sts, k2, (YO) twice, ssk, (YO) twice, CDD, (YO) twice, k2.
Row 11: *k3, (YO) twice, CDD, (YO) twice, k4, (p1, k1) twice; rep from * to last 9 sts, k3, (YO) twice, CDD, (YO) twice, k3.
Row 12: rep row 2.
Row 13: rep row 1.
Row 14: rep row 2.

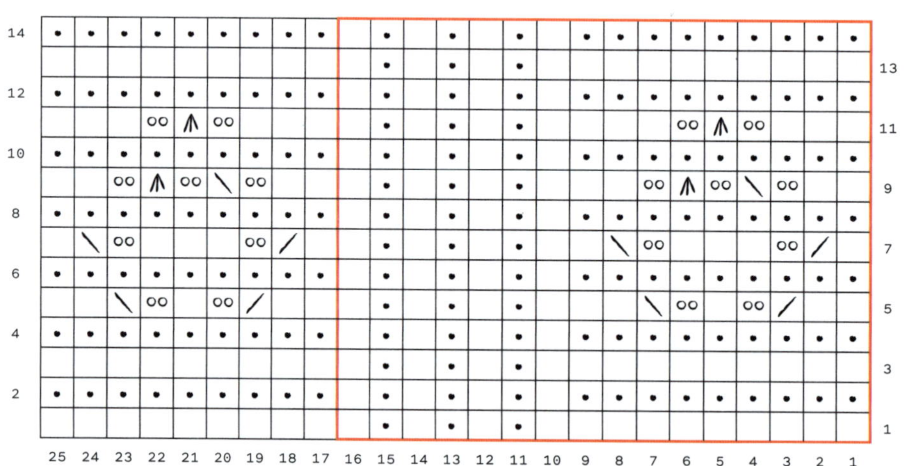

BOUSTA SOCKS

by Gudrun Johnston

We are always glad to have some hand-knitted socks to pad around Burrastow Cottage. This is actually the first time I have written a sock pattern, and what immediately came to mind was using the same motif from my Bousta Beanie hat (which can be found on Ravelry). As with the hat, these socks feature a short and easy pattern repeat that makes for a good beginner colourwork project; folks new to sock knitting should find these accessible, too. A gradient-style yarn will shine in this pattern.

CONSTRUCTION

These colourwork socks are worked from the cuff down with an afterthought heel construction. The colourwork is charted. Leg and foot lengths are customizable; the heel may be completed before the foot and toe in order to achieve the correct foot length (note that adjustments in length will affect total yarn quantity required). The toe stitches are grafted together.

SIZES

1(2, 3)

FINISHED MEASUREMENTS

20.5(23, 25.5)cm/8(9, 10)in foot circumference of finished sock

Choose a size that will result in approx. 2.5cm (1in) of negative ease based on the wearer's foot circumference. Leg and foot lengths are adjustable.

MATERIALS

Yarn: 4-ply (fingering) weight yarn in the following approx. amounts:
MC: 230(260, 285)m/250(280, 310)yds
CC: 130(150, 160)m/140(160, 175)yds

Note: yarn quantity may vary depending on leg length, foot length and yarn type used.

Shown in:
MC: Retrosaria Mondim (100% Portuguese wool; 100g/3½oz/3½oz/385m/421yds) in shade 301
CC: Spincycle Yarns Dyed In The Wool (100% American wool; 50g/1¾oz/183m/200yds) in shade Close Call
MC, CC: 1 skein each for all sizes (see yarn quantity note above)

Needles:
Smaller (for Ribbing, Heel and Toe): 2.25mm (UK 13, US 1) set of DPNs*
Larger (for Colourwork): 2.75mm (UK 12, US 2) set of DPNs*

**For small circumference in the round; alternatively, use a long circular with the Magic Loop method.*

Notions: 2 stitch markers, 4-ply (fingering) weight smooth waste yarn in a contrasting colour, tapestry needle

TENSION/GAUGE

32 sts and 40 rounds = 10cm (4in) over Fair Isle Pattern worked in the round using larger needle after blocking

PATTERN NOTES

See pattern for how to customize leg and foot lengths. If lengthening either, more yarn may be required.

If using a gradient yarn, consider winding two separate balls so that the colour gradients match in each sock.

See Techniques for additional instructions on the following: German Twisted Cast-On, Long-Tail Cast-On, Afterthought Heels, Grafting.

1 st using the Long-Tail Cast-On, CO 1 st using the German Twisted Cast-On; rep from * until all sts are cast on.

PM for BOR and join for working in the round, being careful not to twist.

Rib Round: *k1, p1; rep from * to end of rnd. Work rib round a total of 13 times or until ribbing measures 2.5cm (1in) from cast-on edge.

Change to larger needle(s) and knit 1 rnd with MC.

Next Round: repeat 4 sts from round 1 of Fair Isle Chart to end of rnd.

Last rnd sets chart pattern. Continue to work from chart until rounds 1–14 have been worked a total of three times and then work rounds 1–7 one more time (or work until desired leg length), recording last chart rnd worked.

HEEL PLACEMENT

Work next rnd of chart for 32(36, 40) sts.

Using waste yarn, knit to BOR. Break waste yarn, leaving a tail. Slip the sts worked in waste yarn back to the LHN pwise.

Now using the working yarns, continue working the current chart rnd across the waste yarn sts to BOR. You have inserted half a rnd of waste yarn to the fabric that will be used later to work the heel.

Continue in chart pattern for approx. 5–7.5cm (2–3in) of the foot. Leave needle(s) and yarns in place and make a note of which chart rnd you have ended on.

Note: Working the heel next before finishing the foot will allow you to try it on for a more accurate fit. If you prefer, you can complete the sock's foot and toe and then work the heel; to do so, skip ahead to Foot.

HEEL

Note: you are now going to pick up sts above and below the waste yarn sts; the sts will be placed on needles without being worked (see Techniques for working the Afterthought Heel).

Using smaller needle(s), pick up the right leg of the first st directly below the waste yarn. Continue placing the right leg of every st below the waste yarn on your needle(s), then pick up 1 extra st in the corner for a total of 33(37, 41) sts. The extra st helps to close the gap created by the waste yarn.

Next, pick up the right leg of every st directly above the waste yarn, including 1 extra st in the opposite corner from before (66(74, 82) sts now on needle(s)).

Using a tapestry needle, tease out one end of the waste yarn and unravel the waste yarn sts until waste yarn is removed, making sure that all sts are safely on needles.

Note: you may notice that the CC floats on one half of the picked up stitches look like large loops and not like a regular stitch (depending on when you stopped in the chart). When you come to knit these just make sure to keep the float to the back of the work and the CC stitch will resume the correct position.

Rejoin MC, PM for BOR and knit 3 rnds using smaller needle(s) (note that you may need to hold CC sts in place as you knit them on the first rnd).

Set-up Round: *k2tog, k29(33, 37) sts, k2tog, PM; rep from * one more time (the second repeat will not require a new marker to be placed as the BOR marker is here) (4 sts dec).

Round 1: knit.
Round 2: *k2tog, knit to 2 sts before marker, k2tog; rep from * one more time (4 sts dec).
Repeat rounds 1 and 2 until 26(30, 34) sts total rem.

Using MC, graft the two sets of 13(15, 17) sts together to close the heel.

FOOT

Return to the live sts of the main body of foot and resume working chart pattern at correct rnd (64(72, 80) sts).

Work until foot measures approx. 4(4.5, 5)cm/ 1½(1¾, 2)in short of desired length, ending on either round 7 or 14 of chart if possible.

Break CC yarn.

TOE

Change to smaller needle(s) and continue with MC.

Set-up Round: *k2tog, k28(32, 36), k2tog, PM; rep from * one more time (the second repeat will not require a new marker to be placed as the BOR marker is here) (4 sts dec).

Round 1: knit.
Round 2: *k2tog, knit to 2 sts before marker, k2tog; rep from * one more time (4 sts dec).
Repeat rounds 1 and 2 until 24(28, 32) sts total rem.

Graft the two sets of 12(14, 16) sts together to close the toe.

FINISHING

If you elected to complete the foot and toe before working the heel, return to Heel and work as directed.

Repeat pattern for second sock.

Weave in all ends, using ends to close any holes from where heel sts were picked up. Soak socks in cool water and a gentle wool wash (optional). Remove excess water by carefully squeezing (not wringing) and then press between towels. Block to size.

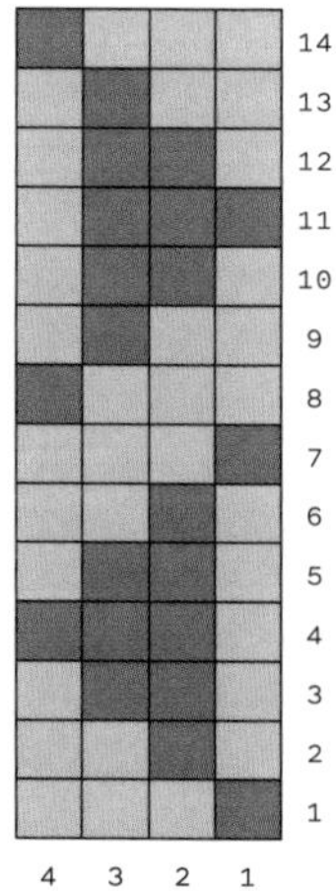

LUCKY LINES PULLOVER

by Gudrun Johnston

Upon finishing this sweater, I was struck by how much it reminded me of tangled lines of seaweed waving about in the water.

'Lucky Lines' is a Shetland term used for sea lace, a type of seaweed that is found in shallow water and attaches itself to the sea bed by a loop. Who doesn't want to knit a lucky sweater!

CONSTRUCTION

This garment is worked in one piece from the bottom up. The body is worked in the round to the underarm, then placed on hold. Sleeves are worked in the round beginning with the cuff and then joined with the body at underarm for the yoke. The yoke has raglan shaping. Short Rows are worked before the yoke's lace pattern to raise the back of the sweater for a better fitting neckline. The lace pattern is charted and written. Hem, cuffs and neck are worked in 2×2 rib. Body and sleeve lengths can easily be adjusted (note that adjustments in length will affect total yarn quantity required).

SIZES

1(2, 3, 4, 5)(6, 7, 8, 9, 10)

FINISHED MEASUREMENTS

Chest circumference: 87.5(93.5, 102.5, 108.5, 114.5)(120.5, 126.5, 134, 141.5, 147.5)cm/34½(36¾, 40¼, 42¾, 45)(47½, 49¾, 52¾, 55¾, 58)in
Side length from underarm: 25(25, 25, 25, 25)(25, 25, 25, 25, 25)cm/9¾ (9¾, 9¾, 9¾, 9¾)(9¾, 9¾, 9¾, 9¾, 9¾)in
Front yoke depth: 19(19, 19, 21.5, 21.5)(23, 23, 23.5, 25.5, 25.5)cm/7½ (7½, 7½, 8½, 8½)(9, 9, 9¼, 10, 10)in
Back yoke depth: 22.5(22.5, 23, 25.5, 25.5)(27.5, 27.5, 28.5, 30.5, 30.5)cm/8¾(8¾, 9, 10, 10)(10¾, 10¾, 11¼, 12, 12)in
Sleeve length from underarm: 31.5(31.5, 31.5, 31.5, 31.5)(31.5, 31.5, 31.5, 31.5, 31.5)cm/12¼(12¼, 12¼, 12¼, 12¼)(12¼, 12¼, 12¼, 12¼, 12¼)in
Upper sleeve circumference: 30(30, 32, 32.5, 35)(36, 39.5, 41.5, 42, 44)cm/11¾(11¾, 12½, 13, 13¾)(14¼, 15½, 16¼, 16½, 17¼)in
Neck circumference): 48(48, 51.5, 51.5, 51.5)(51.5, 55.5, 55.5, 59, 59)cm/19(19, 20¼, 20¼, 20¼)(20¼, 21¾, 21¾, 23¼, 23¼)in

Designed to be worn with approx. 5–10cm (2–4in) of positive ease. Model is wearing size 3 with approx. 7.5cm (3in) of positive ease.

MATERIALS

Yarn: 4-ply (light fingering) weight yarn in the following approx. amount:
905(960, 1055, 1120, 1175)(1245, 1305, 1380, 1460, 1520)m/990(1050, 1150, 1225, 1285)(1360, 1425, 1510, 1595, 1660)yds

Shown in: Holst Garn Supersoft (100% wool; 50g/1¾oz/287m/314yds) in shade 064 Tundra
4(4, 4, 5, 5)(5, 5, 5, 6, 6) balls

Needles:
Ribbing: 3.25mm (UK 10, US 3) circular needle, 40cm (16in) and 80cm (32in) or 100cm (40in) length as well as 3.25mm (UK 10, US 3) set of DPNs*
Main: 3.5mm (UK 10/9, US 4) circular needle, 60cm (24in) length and 80cm (32in) or 100cm (40in) length as well as 3.5mm (UK 10/9, US 4) set of DPNs*

**For small circumference in the round; alternatively, use a long circular with the Magic Loop method.*

Notions: 6 markers (1 for BOR, 3 for raglan, 2 for short rows), waste yarn, tapestry needle

TENSION/GAUGE

27 sts and 34 rounds = 10cm (4in) over Stocking (Stockinette) Stitch worked in the round using main needle, after blocking

27 sts and 35 rounds = 10cm (4in) over Chart A Pattern worked in the round using main needle, after blocking

22 sts and 38 rounds = 10cm (4in) over 2×2 ribbing worked in the round using ribbing needle, after blocking

PATTERN NOTES

The stitch pattern may be worked from either charted or written instructions. The written instructions can be found on our Bookmarked Hub – www.bookmarkedhub.com

The German Short Row method is used to shape the lower back yoke.

See pattern for how to lengthen body and/or sleeves (more yarn required).

See Techniques for additional instructions on the following: German Twisted Cast-On, Long-Tail Cast-On, German Short Rows, Grafting.

INSTRUCTIONS

BODY

Using longer circular ribbing needle, CO 232(248, 272, 288, 304)(320, 336, 356, 376, 392) sts as follows (alternatively, use only the Long-Tail Cast-On):
Make a slip knot and place it on needle as the first st, CO 1 st using the Long-Tail Cast-On, CO 2 sts using the German Twisted Cast-On, *CO 2 sts using the Long-Tail Cast-On, CO 2 sts using the German Twisted Cast-On; rep from * until all sts are cast on.

PM for BOR and join for working in the round, being careful not to twist.

Rib Round: *k2, p2; rep from * to end of rnd.
Work rib round a total of 12 times or until ribbing measures 3cm (1¼in) from cast on edge.

Change to longer main circular needle.

Work in st st until body measures 25cm (9¾in) from cast on edge (or to desired length) AND at the same time when working the last rnd, place underarm sts on waste yarn as follows:

K121(129, 143, 152, 161)(170, 180, 192, 203, 212) sts, place last 10(10, 14, 16, 18)(20, 24, 28, 30, 32) sts just worked onto waste yarn for first underarm, knit to end. Place last 5(5, 7, 8, 9)(10, 12, 14, 15, 16) sts just worked at end of rnd and the first 5 (5, 7, 8, 9) (10, 12, 14, 15, 16) sts at the beginning of the rnd onto waste yarn for second underarm (212(228, 244, 256, 268)(280, 288, 300, 316, 328) sts rem for body).

Break yarn leaving body sts on the needle.

SLEEVE (MAKE TWO)

Using ribbing needle (DPNs or circular if using Magic Loop), CO 60(60, 64, 64, 68)(68, 72, 76, 80, 84) sts as follows (alternatively, use only the Long-Tail Cast-On):
Make a slip knot and place it on needle as the first st, CO 1 st using the Long-Tail Cast-On, CO 2 sts using the German Twisted Cast-On, *CO 2 sts using the Long-Tail Cast-On, CO 2 sts using the German Twisted Cast-On; rep from * until all sts are cast on.

PM for BOR and join for working in the round, being careful not to twist.

Rib Round: *k2, p2; rep from * to end of rnd.
Work rib round a total of 12 times or until ribbing measures 3cm (1¼in) from cast on edge.

Change to main needle (either DPNs or circular if using Magic Loop).

Work in st st in the round for 8(8, 8, 8, 8)(8, 7, 7, 7, 7) rnds.

Inc Round: k2, M1L, knit to last 2 sts, M1R, k2 (2 sts inc).

Continue working in st st in the round and repeat Inc round every 10th(10th, 10th, 8th, 8th)(6th, 6th, 5th, 6th, 6th) rnd 3(3, 3, 6, 6)(13, 5, 16, 5, 5) more times, then every 8th(8th, 8th, 6th, 6th)(–, 5th, –, 5th, 5th) rnd 6 (6, 6, 5, 5) (–, 10, –, 10, 10) more time(s) (20(20, 20, 24, 24)(28, 32, 34, 32, 32) sts inc; 80(80, 84, 88, 92)(96, 104, 110, 112, 116) sts).

Work in st st in the round without shaping for 8(8, 8, 8, 8)(8, 7, 7, 7, 7) rounds or until sleeve measures 31cm (12¼in) from cast on edge.

Break yarn leaving a tail.

Place last 5(5, 7, 8, 9)(10, 12, 14, 15, 16) sts just worked at end of rnd and the first 5(5, 7, 8, 9)(10, 12, 14, 15, 16) sts at the beginning of the rnd onto waste yarn for underarm (70 (70, 70, 72, 74) (76, 80, 82, 82, 84) sts rem for sleeve).

YOKE

Note: before beginning the yoke, you will need 6 markers: 1 for BOR at back left shoulder (also serving as a raglan marker), 3 raglan markers and 2 short row markers (noted as A and B); make sure you know which marker is which.

Yoke Union Round: with body sts still on circular needle, PM for BOR/raglan, k70(70, 70, 72, 74)(76, 80, 82, 82, 84) sts of left sleeve, PM for raglan, k40(42, 44, 46, 48)(50, 52, 54, 56, 58) sts of front, place short row marker A, k26(30, 34, 36, 38)(40, 40, 42, 46, 48) centre front neck sts, place short row marker B, k40(42, 44, 46, 48)(50, 52, 54, 56, 58) rem sts of front, PM for raglan, k70(70, 70, 72, 74)(76, 80, 82, 82, 84) sts of right sleeve, PM for raglan, k106(114, 122, 128, 134)(140, 144, 150, 158, 164) sts of back (352 (368, 384, 400, 416) (432, 448, 464, 480, 496) sts).

Shape Raglans; Shape Back Yoke with German Short Rows

Note: change to shorter circular main needle (same size) as needed while working yoke.

Short Row 1 (RS): knit to short row marker A on left front, turn.

Short Row 2 (WS): DS, purl to short row marker B on right front (slipping other markers as you come to them), turn.

Short Row 3 (Raglan Dec Row): DS, *knit to 3 sts before next raglan marker, ssk, k1, SM, k1, k2tog; rep from * three more times, knit to 8(8, 7, 7, 7)(6, 6, 6, 6, 6) sts before last turning point (counting DS as 1 st), turn (8 sts dec).

Short Row 4: DS, purl to 8(8, 7, 7, 7)(6, 6, 6, 6, 6) sts before last turning point, turn.

Repeat Short Rows 3 and 4 another 3(3, 4, 4, 4)(5, 5, 6, 6, 6) times (320(336, 344, 360, 376)(384, 400, 408, 424, 440) sts rem).

Next Round (Raglan Dec Round): DS, *knit to 3 sts before raglan marker, ssk, k1, SM, k1, k2tog; rep from * three more times across next 3 raglan markers, work to first DS on left front and k2tog the two legs of the DS to close, resolve rem DSs on left front as you come to them in the same way until you reach short row marker A, remove short row marker A, knit across to 1 st before short row marker B, slip next st kwise, remove short row marker B, knit the first leg of the DS tbl then psso, knit the second leg of the DS tbl, close rem DSs on the right front in the same way (technique attributed to Patty Lyons), knit to BOR marker (312(328, 336, 352, 368)(376, 392, 400, 416, 432) total sts: 60(60, 58, 60, 62)(62, 66, 66, 66, 68) sleeve sts and 96(104, 110, 116, 122)(126, 130, 134, 142, 148) sts each front and back).

Sizes 1 and 3
Proceed to All Sizes.

Sizes 2, 4, 5, 6, 7, 8, 9 and 10
Note: raglan shaping continues for these sizes.

Next Round: knit.
Next Round (Raglan Dec Round): *k1, k2tog, knit to 3 sts before raglan marker, ssk, k1, sm; rep from * three more times (8 sts dec).
Repeat last 2 rnds –(1, –, 1, 0)(1, 0, 1, 0, 2) more time(s) (–(312, –, 336, 360)(360, 384, 384, 408, 408) sts rem).

All Sizes
Next Round: knit, removing raglan markers (312(312, 336, 336, 360)(360, 384, 384, 408, 408) sts).

Work in st st in the round without shaping for 4(0, 4, 8, 10)(12, 14, 14, 22, 18) more rnd(s), or until yoke measures 5(5, 5, 7.5, 7.5)(9.5, 9.5, 11, 12.5, 12.5)cm/2(2, 2, 3, 3)(3¾, 3¾, 4¼, 5, 5)in from the centre back yoke joining round.

Next Round: work round 1 of Chart A, working rep a total of 13(13, 14, 14, 15)(15, 16, 16, 17, 17) times, to end of rnd.

Last rnd sets Chart A pattern. Continue to work from Chart A until round 30 is complete.

Next Round: work round 1 of Chart B, working rep a total of 13(13, 14, 14, 15)(15, 16, 16, 17, 17) times, to end of rnd. (*Note:* round 1 will decrease 2 sts per repeat.)

Last rnd sets Chart B pattern. Continue to work from Chart B until round 30 is complete; see chart or written instructions regarding BOR shift at end of round 28 (104(104, 112, 112, 120)(120, 128, 128, 136, 136) sts rem).

Sizes 1–4
Proceed to All Sizes.

Sizes 5–10
Next Round (Dec Round): k–(–, –, –, 13)(13, 14, 14, 15, 15), k2tog; rep from * to end of rnd (8 sts dec; –(–, –, –, 112)(112, 120, 120, 128, 128) sts rem).

All Sizes
Change to shorter circular ribbing needle.

Rib Round: *k2, p2; rep from * to end of rnd.
Work rib round a total of five times.

Cast (bind) off all sts in rib pattern.

FINISHING

Graft underarm sts together. Weave in ends. Soak sweater in cool water and a gentle wool wash (optional) for at least 20 minutes. Remove excess water from fabric by carefully squeezing (not wringing) and then press between towels. Block to finished measurements.

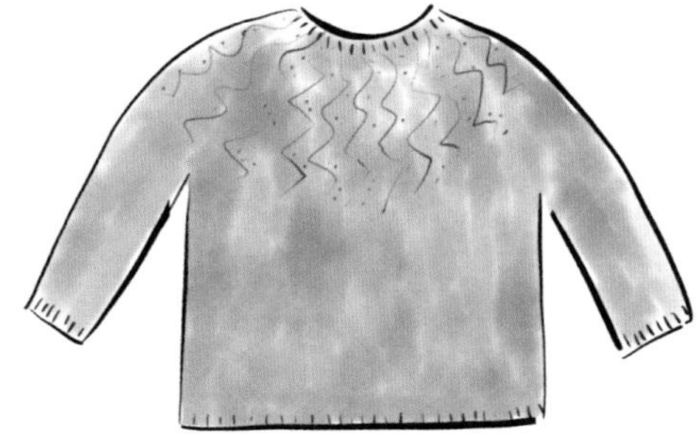

CHART A

																								30
λ			O		O			λ			O		O			λ			O		O			29
																								28
λ			O		O			λ			O		O			λ			O		O			27
																								26
λ			O		O			λ			O		O			λ			O		O			25
																								24
λ			O		O			λ			O		O			λ			O		O			23
																								22
λ			O		O			λ			O		O			λ			O		O			21
																								20
O		O			λ			O		O			λ			O		O			λ			19
																								18
O		O			λ			O		O			λ			O		O			λ			17
																								16
O		O			λ			O		O			λ			O		O			λ			15
																								14
O		O			λ			O		O			λ			O		O			λ			13
																								12
O		O			λ			O		O			λ			O		O			λ			11
																								10
								λ			O		O											9
																								8
								λ			O		O											7
																								6
								λ			O		O											5
																								4
								λ			O		O											3
																								2
								λ			O		O											1
24	23	22	21	20	19	18	17	16	15	14	13	12	11	10	9	8	7	6	5	4	3	2	1	

CHART B

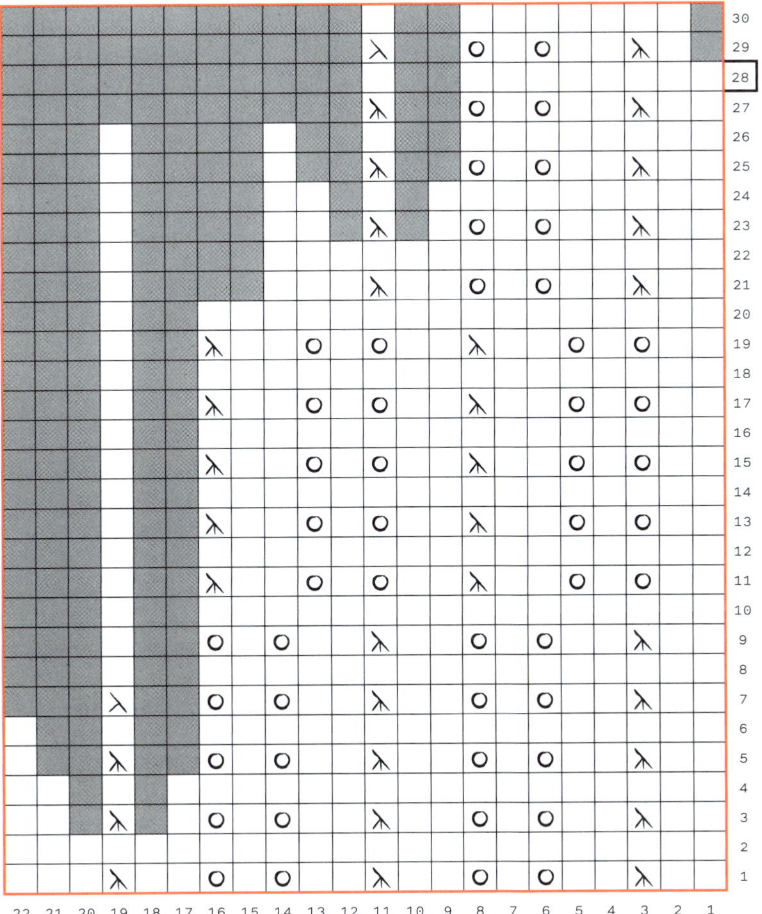

AT END OF ROUND 28 AND BEFORE STARTING ROUND 29, REMOVE BOR MARKER, SLIP NEXT ST PURLWISE TO RH NEEDLE, REPLACE BOR MARKER.

WEST IS BEST

by Mary Jane Mucklestone

It's pure pleasure waking up in our rooms at Burrastow Guesthouse. Raucous seabirds announce the day, frisking ponies snort their approval, and if we're lucky, the warm summer sun beams down upon the waters of Vaila Sound just outside our door. Bliss. As tempting as it is to loll away the morning at 'home', adventure beckons! There are countless places to explore here in our corner of the Westside. Just the mention of Jamieson's spinning mill, and any lingering thoughts of a lie-in are abandoned.

From the village of Walls, we drive through seemingly empty moorland but look closely, and you'll see the traces of human habitation reaching back 5,000 years! When we're travelling around the islands, I always follow along on Ordnance Survey maps. The maps indicate road information, interesting land and water features, and my favourite – archaeological elements. It's fun to try to read the landscape for burnt mounds, ancient stone cairns, and Neolithic field systems. Small lochs carved by ancient glaciers pepper this stretch of our drive. We will almost certainly see graceful water lilies or an elegant pair of swans, and we might even spy a crannog – a neolithic dwelling built in one of the lochs.

Heading down the hill into the community of Sandness, a gorgeous view of St Magnus Bay and the island of Papa Stour spreads out before us. Just past Turrifield, an organic farm, we don our Bousta Beanies designed by Gudrun and gather around the Bousta road sign for a group portrait.

Family-owned Jamieson's of Shetland (not to be confused with the other main yarn company, Jamieson & Smith) has been in the wool business for five generations. They opened the mill in the early 80s, realizing their dream of manufacturing entirely Shetland-made wool products; it's the only commercial woollen mill on the islands. They buy fleeces directly from crofters and do all the production involved in their 100% Shetland wool hand-knitting yarn. They also make finished sweaters on sophisticated knitting machines. But it doesn't stop there: Jamieson's also weaves fine tweed fabric on vintage looms, creating beautiful wool blankets and fabric for the fashion industry.

Today, we are fortunate to get a tour of the mill (if you hope to visit, check if tours are currently available). Manager Garry Jamieson shows us around and explains the entire process from grading, scouring, and dyeing fleece in-the-wool, then colour blending (for their 220 colours) in what seems like a huge whooshing cupboard, followed by carding, spinning, twisting and finally balling and labelling the yarn. And then to the mill shop! We have learnt not to rush this part of the visit. In addition to a stunning 'wall of wool' with all the colours and styles of yarn, there are sweaters, scarves and blankets for sale. And, if the mills shop is closed, you can also do your shopping at their fabulous shop in Lerwick.

Just behind the mill is the start of one of our favourite hikes. It's a challenge to climb Sandness Hill, the highest point in the Westside, but entirely worth it to see its splendid 360° view of the surrounding countryside, ocean, and islands. Most impressive is Foula, lying 24km (15mi) off the coast, with a heart-stopping silhouette like a ship sailing off into the Atlantic. We continue onwards to Bankshead, vertigo-inducing cliffs high above the bay of Deepdale. It's a spectacular setting with sea stacks, arches and impossibly turquoise waters. Look closely; you might spot seaweed-snacking sheep on the beach! It's an excellent beach for swimming if you dare travel the treacherous path down. With our group, we stay well away from the cliffs and stop halfway down the slope to enjoy our packed lunch; comfortably leaning into the heather, the valley is so steep it's like sitting in a chair.

Rejuvenated, we carry on through breathtaking scenery to the beach at Dale of Walls, where we meet our ride back to Burrastow. It's a lovely drive along a single-track road ablaze with wildflowers. Sheep of many different colours dot the fields – and very often the road as well! If approached on foot, Shetland sheep usually turn tail and run, yet they seem strangely unperturbed by passing cars and can be found napping on the tarmac.

An impressive working peat bank, where Shetlanders still cut peat for fuel, is a highlight of this stretch of road. We take our last stop here to admire the hard work and skill of the task. A relaxing evening is promised, sharing memories of the wonders of our day. As they say on the Westside, West is best!

ISLAND TO ISLAND VEST

by Mary Jane Mucklestone

It's fun to have fellow travellers who are professionals or enthusiasts of disciplines different from your own. One member of our group had a passion for geology that was infectious! Shetland is a UNESCO Global Geopark, and many visitors come solely for the rocks. Commenting that some of the stones look just like some I collect in Maine, our friend confirmed that eons ago, the two places were connected! To renew the union, I use Nash Island Maine wool in this Fair Isle vest.

The pattern motifs on even- and odd-numbered sizes create slightly different shoulder alignments. Even sizes meet diamond-to-diamond, while the motifs on odd-numbered sizes align in a zigzag pattern. In some cases, you may choose to remove or add a row to fine-tune the join and achieve the look you prefer.

CONSTRUCTION

This vest's body is worked bottom up in the round, beginning with a deep 1×1 ribbed hem, followed by a Fair Isle pattern worked to the shoulders. Steek stitches bridge the gaps for the neckline and armholes. Once the neckline shaping is complete, the shoulder stitches are joined with a Three-Needle Cast- (Bind-) Off. Stitches are picked up around the openings and worked in a 1×1 ribbed edging.

SIZES

1(2, 3, 4, 5)(6, 7, 8, 9)

FINISHED MEASUREMENTS

Chest circumference: 78(87, 96, 105, 113)(122, 131, 139, 148)cm/30¾(34¼, 37¾, 41¼, 44½)(48, 51½, 54¾, 58¼)in
Hip circumference: 59(66, 73, 79.5, 86.5)(93.5, 99.5, 106.5, 113.5)cm/23¼(26, 28¾, 31¼, 34)(36¾, 39¼, 42, 44¾)in
Back neck width: 17(18, 18, 18, 18.5)(21.5, 21.5, 22, 23.5)cm/6¾(7, 7, 7, 7¼)(8½, 8½, 8¾, 9¼)in
Cross-back width: 28.5(29, 31, 32.5, 33)(36, 36, 38, 39.5)cm/11¼(11½, 12¼, 12¾, 13)(14¼, 14¼, 15, 15½)in
Shoulder width: 5.5(5.5, 6.5, 7, 7)(7, 7, 7.5, 7.5)cm/2¼(2¼, 2½, 2¾, 2¾)(2¾, 2¾, 3, 3)in
Yoke depth: 21(21.5, 22, 23, 24)(25, 25.5, 25.5, 26.5)cm/8¼(8½, 8¾, 9, 9½)(9¾, 10, 10, 10½)in
Front neck drop: 12(12.5, 13.5, 11.5, 10.5)(11, 11.5, 11.5, 10.5)cm/4¾(5, 5¼, 4¾, 4¼)(4½, 4¾, 4¾, 4¼)in
Body length: 54(54.5, 55, 56, 57)(58, 58.5, 58.5, 59.5)cm/21¼(21½, 21¾, 22, 22½)(22¾, 23, 23, 23½)in
Side length from underarm: 33(33, 33, 33, 33)(33, 33, 33, 33)cm/13(13, 13, 13, 13)(13, 13, 13, 13)in

Designed to be worn with approx. 0–5cm (0–2in) of negative ease. Model is wearing size 2 with no ease.

MATERIALS

Yarn: 5-ply (sport) weight yarn in the following approx. amounts:
MC: 270(290, 320, 345, 380)(410, 435, 455, 495)m/295(320, 350, 380, 415)(450, 475, 500, 540)yds
CC1: 100(110, 120, 135, 140)(155, 165, 175, 185)m/110(120, 130, 145, 155)(170, 180, 190, 200)yds
CC2: 225(240, 265, 290, 310)(340, 355, 380, 405)m/245(265, 290, 315, 340)(370, 390, 415, 445)yds
CC3: 80(85, 95, 105, 115)(125, 130, 135, 145)m/90(95, 105, 115, 125)(135, 140, 150, 160)yds

Shown in: Nash Island Tide (100% Wild Maine Island wool; 50g/1¾oz/160m/175yds) in shades Raven (MC), Seaweed (CC1), Moss (CC2), and Lichen (CC3)
MC: 2(2, 3, 3, 3)(3, 3, 3, 4) skeins
CC1: 1(1, 1, 1, 1)(1, 2, 2, 2) skeins
CC2: 2(2, 2, 2, 2)(3, 3, 3, 3) skeins
CC3: 1(1, 1, 1, 1)(1, 1, 1, 1) skein

Needles:
Ribbing: 2.25mm (UK 13, US 1) circular needle, 40cm (16in) and 60–80cm (24–30in) length
Main: 3.25mm (UK 10, US 3) circular needle, 40cm (16in) and 60–80cm (24–30in) length

Notions: 4 stitch holders or waste yarn, stitch markers of different colours, locking ring markers or safety pins, tapestry needle, T-pins for blocking, sharp scissors

For reinforcing steeks, use one of the following (see Techniques for additional information):
For crocheted steeks: 3.25mm (UK 10, D-3) crochet hook and sturdy 5-ply (sport) weight yarn
For machine-sewn steeks: sewing machine and sturdy thread
For hand-stitched steeks: a sewing needle and sturdy thread

TENSION/GAUGE

28 sts and 32 rounds = 10cm (4in) over Fair Isle Pattern worked in the round using main needle, after blocking

32 sts and 36 rounds = 10cm (4in) over 1×1 Ribbing worked in the round using ribbing needle, after blocking

PATTERN NOTES

When working this Fair Isle pattern, hold the MC to the left of the other colour, regardless of how you hold your yarn. The float of the MC yarn should lie below the float of the CC yarn on the WS.

See Steek Chart for stripe patterning when working neck and armhole steeks; note that BOR is at centre of steek. Maintaining the steek striping as indicated provides a clear, 2-stitch centre line in background colour (CC) for cutting the steeks open as well as a clear, unobtrusive edge in pattern colour (MC) for picking up the neckband and sleeve edging.

Charts are worked in the round, from right to left, in knit with the exception of finishing the shoulders when the charts are worked flat and read from right to left on RS (knit) rows and from left to right on WS (purl) rows.

You can customize the length of your vest by adding or subtracting pattern rounds before casting on for armhole or neck steeks, but keep in mind that adjusting the pattern rounds will affect where the pattern ends at top shoulder. Note that any adjustments in length will also affect the total yarn quantity required.

See Techniques for additional instructions on the following: Steeks, Backwards Loop Cast-On, Three-Needle Cast- (Bind-) Off.

INSTRUCTIONS

BODY

With longer ribbing needle and MC, CO 210(234, 258, 282, 306)(330, 354, 378, 402) sts using your preferred stretchy cast-on.

PM for BOR and join for working in the round, being careful not to twist.

Rib Round: *k1, p1; rep from * to end of rnd. Work rib round until ribbing measures 11.5cm (4½in) from cast on edge.

Inc Round: *k35(39, 43, 47, 51)(55, 59, 63, 67), M1L; rep from * to end of rnd (6 sts inc; 216(240, 264, 288, 312)(336, 360, 384, 408) sts).

Change to longer main needle and join CC1.

Set-up Round: *k1 with CC1, k1 with MC; rep from * to end of rnd.

Begin working from the Vest Chart as follows, changing colours as indicated:
Next Round: work across 8 sts from round 1 of Vest Chart to end of rnd.
Last rnd sets chart pattern. Work Vest Chart rounds 1–32 two times. Work rounds 1–3 from Vest Chart one more time.

After 67 Vest Chart rnds worked, vest measures approx. 33cm (13in) from cast on edge to beginning of armhole. Check length and work more chart rnds as needed to reach desired length. If additional rnds are worked, note last rnd worked and adjust the following instructions regarding which rnd to work next accordingly.

Sizes 1, 3, 4, 5, 7, 8 and 9
Centre the diamond motif in the front by adjusting the BOR position as follows:
Next Round (round 4 if length is not adjusted): remove BOR marker, work 6(–, 2, 4, 6)(–, 2, 4, 6) sts in pattern, PM for new BOR, work in pattern to new BOR.

All Sizes
Next, underarm sts are placed on hold and steek sts are cast on using the Backwards Loop Cast-On. The Set-up round repositions the BOR to the centre of the left underarm steek sts (with four steek sts on either side of BOR), with additional markers on either side of both underarm steek columns. When working a rnd of the Vest Chart, the same corresponding rnd should be worked of the Steek Chart. When shaping the armholes and upper body, maintain the Fair Isle pattern as established throughout, working decreases in the appropriate colour to keep in pattern.

Set-up Round (round 5 if length is not adjusted): Remove BOR, place 5(5, 7, 7, 8)(10, 11, 13, 14) sts on a st holder, PM for BOR; beginning with columns 5 and 6 of the corresponding rnd of Steek Chart, join each yarn colour with a slip knot (these are the first and second steek sts) and CO 2 more steek sts in pattern, work Vest Chart as established for 97(109, 117, 129, 139)(147, 157, 165, 175) sts, PM, place next 11(11, 15, 15, 17)(21, 23, 27, 29) sts on a stitch holder, CO 8 steek sts according to same rnd of Steek Chart, PM, work Vest Chart as established for 97(109, 117, 129, 139 (147, 157, 165, 175) sts, slip rem 6(6, 8, 8, 9)(11, 12, 14, 15) sts to the first st holder, PM, CO 4 steek sts in pattern according to same rnd of Steek Chart (the first four columns of the chart) (210(234, 250, 274, 294)(310, 330, 346, 366) total sts: 97(109, 117, 129, 139)(147, 157, 165, 175) sts each front and back and two 8-st underarm steeks).

Shape Armholes
Armhole Dec Round: beginning with column 5 of Steek Chart, work next rnd of Steek Chart to marker, *SM, k2tog, work in pattern to 2 sts before next marker, ssk, SM, work Steek Chart to marker; rep from * to end of rnd, ending with column 4 of Steek Chart (4 sts dec).
Work Armhole Dec Round a total of 5(8, 10, 12, 14)(14, 17, 18, 20) times (87(93, 97, 105, 111)(119, 123, 129, 135) sts each front and back).

Round 1: work next rnd from charts without decreasing.
Round 2 (Dec Round): work Armhole Dec Round (4 sts dec).
Work the last 2 rnds a total of 4(6, 6, 8, 10)(10, 12, 12, 13) times (79(81, 85, 89, 91)(99, 99, 105, 109) sts rem for each front and back).

Armhole shaping is now complete. Work in chart patterns as established until piece measures approx. 9(9, 9, 11, 14)(14, 14, 16, 16)cm/3½(3½, 3½, 4¼, 5½)(5½, 5½, 6¼, 6¼)in from the beginning of armhole shaping. Chart rounds 7, 16, 23 and 32 are good stopping points before beginning front neck shaping.

Steek Set-up for Shaping Front Neck
Set-up Round: work in pattern for 27(28, 29, 31, 31)(32, 32, 34, 34) left front neck sts, cast (bind) off 25(25, 27, 27, 29)(35, 35, 37, 41) front neck sts, PM, CO 8 steek sts for front neck following corresponding rnd of Steek Chart, PM, work in pattern to BOR (157(161, 167, 175, 177)(187, 187, 197, 201) total sts: 27(28, 29, 31, 31)(32, 32, 34, 34) sts each front, 79(81, 85, 89, 91)(99, 99, 105, 109) back sts and three 8-st steeks).

Neck Dec Round: work steek to marker, SM, work in pattern to 2 sts before marker, k2tog, SM, work steek to marker, SM, ssk, work in pattern to end (2 sts dec, 1 st per neck edge).
Work Neck Dec Round rnd a total of five times (22(23, 24, 26, 26)(27, 27, 29, 29) sts rem for each front).

Round 1: work next rnd from charts without decreasing.
Round 2 (Dec Round): work Neck Dec Round (2 sts dec, 1 st per neck edge).
Work the last 2 rnds a total of five times (17(18, 19, 21, 21)(22, 22, 24, 24) sts rem for each front).

Rounds 1 and 2: work next rnd from charts without decreasing.
Round 3 (Dec Round): work Neck Dec Round (2 sts dec, 1 st per neck edge).
Work last 3 rnds a total of 2(3, 2, 2, 2)(3, 3, 3, 3) times (15(15, 17, 19, 19)(19, 19, 21, 21) sts rem for each front).

Front neck shaping is now complete. Work until piece measures approx. 19.5(20.5, 21, 21.5, 23)(23.5, 24, 24, 25.5)cm/7¾(8, 8¼, 8½, 9)(9¼, 9½, 9½, 10)in from the beginning of armhole shaping. Back neck shaping is worked over 5 rnds, so you may wish to end your work here 5 rnds short of where you would like the motif to complete at the shoulder (good completion points are rounds 4, 7, 12, 16, 20, 23, 28 or 32).

Shape Back Neck
You will now cast (bind) off the centre 6 sts in each steek column; the rem 2 sts of each steek will become selvedge sts for the shoulders and neck edge.

Next Round: Working in pattern, cast (bind) off 3 steek sts, k1 (this st is already on RHN after cast (bind) off and does not need to be knitted again), RM, work left front shoulder sts to marker, RM, k1, cast (bind) off 6 steek sts, k1 (this st is already on RHN after cast (bind) off and does not need to be knitted again), RM, work right front shoulder sts to marker, RM, k1, cast (bind) off 6 steek sts, k1 (this st is already on RHN after cast (bind) off and does not need to be knitted again), RM, work 16(16, 18, 20, 20)(20, 20, 22, 22) right back shoulder sts, cast (bind) off centre 47(49, 49, 49, 51)(59, 59, 61, 65) back neck sts, work 16(16, 18, 20, 20)(20, 20, 22, 22) left back shoulder sts (the first of these sts is already on RHN after cast (bind) off and doesn't need to be knitted again), RM, k1, cast (bind) off 2 steek sts, break all yarn and pull 1 yarn tail through rem st (17(17, 19, 21, 21)(21, 21, 23, 23) sts rem for each front and back shoulder sts, with 2 selvedge sts (1 on either side) outside of main charted pattern).

Shape Shoulders
Each shoulder section is now worked separately, flat, in st st and Fair Isle pattern. Work rem steek sts (now edge sts) in MC for each row.

Join new yarn and work next 4 rows of Vest Chart flat (k on RS, p on WS, reading chart from right to left on RS and from left to right on WS).

Break yarn and place live sts on st holder.

Repeat for rem shoulder sections.

Reinforce and Cut Steeks
Secure steeks using your preferred method. Cut each steek carefully between the two centre sts (columns 4 and 5 of Steek Chart; before cutting, smooth all ends along each steek towards its centre so that they are trimmed in the cutting process).

Join Shoulders
With MC and holding RSs together, work a Three-Needle Cast- (Bind-) Off for each shoulder.

Wash and block vest to finished measurements before proceeding to finish the neckband and armhole edgings.

Neckband
With RS facing, shorter ribbing needle, and beginning at left back neck, with MC p&k 36(38, 40, 35, 31)(33, 35, 35, 31) sts (approx. 1 st for every row) along the left side of front neck between body and edge/steek sts, p&k 25(25, 27, 27, 29)(35, 35, 37, 41) sts across front neck, p&k 36(38, 40, 35, 31) (33, 35, 35, 31) (approx. 1 st for every row) along the right side of front neck, p&k 5 sts down right back shoulder, p&k 47(49, 49, 49, 51)(59, 59, 61, 65) sts across back neck, p&k 5 sts up left back shoulder (154(160, 166, 156, 152)(170, 174, 178, 178) sts; total st count can vary slightly but should be an even number in order to work 1×1 ribbing).

PM for BOR and join for working in the round.

Rib Round: *k1, p1; rep from * to end of rnd.
Work rib round until neck edging measures 2.5cm (1in).

Cast (bind) off all sts in rib pattern.

Armhole Edgings
Place held sts of one underarm on shorter ribbing needle, slip first 6(6, 8, 8, 9)(11, 12, 14, 15) sts pwise, join MC, k5(5, 7, 7, 8)(10, 11, 13, 14) underarm sts, p&k 61(65, 65, 67, 71)(73, 75, 75, 79) sts (approx. 1 st for every row) from underarm to shoulder seam, p&k 62(64, 66, 68, 72)(74, 76, 76, 80) sts from shoulder seam to underarm, knit across rem 6(6, 8, 8, 9)(11, 12, 14, 15) held underarm sts (134(140, 146, 150, 160)(168, 174, 178, 188) sts; total st count can vary slightly but should be an even number in order to work 1×1 ribbing).

PM for BOR and join for working in the round.

Rib Round: *k1, p1; rep from * to end of rnd.
Work rib round until armhole edging measures 2.5cm (1in).

Cast (bind) off all sts in rib pattern.

Repeat for second armhole edging.

FINISHING

Weave in ends. Trim waste steek sts neatly and fold to WS. Tack down with whipstitch if desired. Wet-block or steam neck and armhole edges if desired.

MC

CC1

CC2

CC3

PC PATTERN COLOUR

BC BACKGROUND COLOUR

PEERIE SHOP CARDI

by Mary Jane Mucklestone

A Lopi cardigan is often all I need for outwear in Shetland. Initially a study in mossy greens, I added the colour of my favourite Sharpie into the mix when I realized how nice it would look with my beloved magenta backpack from The Peerie Shop – which I resisted buying for two years until, finally, I succumbed to its charms. Use a looser-than-typical tension/gauge for a lofty lightweight garment; the magical quality of Icelandic wool puffs up to fill the space.

CONSTRUCTION

This cardigan is worked in the round from the top down to the armholes, then sleeves and body are divided and worked separately in the round to bottom edge. The colourwork is charted; most rounds are worked with two colours, while a few rounds are worked with three. A steek is used to create the centre front opening. Short Rows shape the lower back yoke for a well-fitting neckline. Body hem and sleeve cuffs feature a bit of colourwork and are finished in 1×1 rib. After cutting open the centre front steek, stitches are picked up to work the button band in 1×1 rib. Body and sleeve lengths can be adjusted (note that adjustments in length will affect total yarn quantity required).

SIZES

1(2, 3, 4, 5)(6, 7, 8, 9)

FINISHED MEASUREMENTS

Chest circumference (buttoned): 85(94.5, 105.5, 115, 125.5)(135.5, 147.5, 155.5, 166.5)cm/33½(37¼, 41½, 45¼, 49½)(53¼, 58, 61¼, 65½)in
Neck circumference: 45.5(49, 52, 52, 55)(58.5, 61.5, 65, 68)cm/18(19¼, 20½, 20½, 21¾)(23, 24¼, 25½, 26¾)in
Upper sleeve circumference: 33(36, 37.5, 40.5, 44)(47, 51.5, 51.5, 53.5)cm/13(14¼, 14¾, 16, 17¼)(18½, 20¼, 20¼, 21)in
Cuff circumference: 28(28, 28, 33, 33)(33, 33, 33, 34.5)cm/11(11, 11, 13, 13)(13, 13, 13, 13½)in
Yoke depth (from centre back): 21(21, 22, 23.5, 24)(26.5, 27.5, 28.5, 30)cm/8¼(8¼, 8¾, 9¼, 9½)(10½, 10¾, 11¼, 11¾)in
Underarm to hem: 32.5(32.5, 32.5, 32.5, 32.5)(32.5, 32.5, 32.5, 32.5)cm/12¾(12¾, 12¾, 12¾, 12¾)(12¾, 12¾, 12¾, 12¾)in
Sleeve length from underarm: 43(44.5, 45, 45, 45.5)(47, 47, 48.5, 49.5)cm/17(17½, 17¾, 17¾, 18)(18½, 18½, 19, 19½)in
Body length: 53.5(53.5, 54.5, 56, 56.5)(59, 59.5, 61, 62)cm/21(21, 21½, 22, 22¼)(23¼, 23½, 24, 24½)in

Designed to be worn with 7.5–10cm (3–5in) positive ease at the chest. Model is wearing size 2 with 7.5cm (3in) positive ease.

MATERIALS

Yarn: Aran (10-ply/worsted) weight, woollen spun yarn in the following approx. amounts:
MC: 350(390, 425, 465, 510)(575, 630, 665, 710)m/385(425, 465, 510, 560)(630, 690, 725, 775)yds
CC1: 135(150, 165, 180, 195)(225, 240, 255, 275)m/150(165, 180, 195, 215)(245, 265, 280, 300)yds
CC2: 10(15, 15, 15, 20)(20, 20, 25, 25)m/10(15, 15, 15, 20)(20, 20, 25, 25)yds
CC3: 40(45, 50, 50, 60)(65, 75, 75, 80)m/45(50, 55, 55, 65)(70, 80, 80, 90)yds
CC4: 20(20, 25, 25, 25)(25, 30, 30, 35)m/20(20, 25, 25, 25)(30, 35, 35, 40)yds
CC5: 10(15, 15, 15, 20)(20, 20, 25, 25)m/10(15, 15, 15, 20)(20, 20, 25, 25)yds

Shown in: Ístex Léttlopi (100% Icelandic wool; 50g/1¾oz/1¾oz/100m/109yds) in shades 1405 Bottle Green (MC), 9423 Lagoon Heather (CC1), 1705 Royal Fuchsia (CC2), 1407 Pine Green (CC3), 9421 Celery Green (CC4) and 1417 Frostbite (C5)
MC: 4(4, 5, 5, 6)(6, 7, 7, 8) skeins
CC1: 2(2, 2, 2, 2)(3, 3, 3, 3) skeins
CC2, CC3, CC4 and CC5: 1 skein each

Needles

Smaller (for Ribbing and Button Bands): 5.5mm (UK 5, US 9) circular needle, 40cm (16in) and 80cm (32in) length as well as a set of DPNs*
Larger (for Stocking (Stockinette) Stitch and Colourwork): 6mm (UK 4, US 10) circular needle, 40cm (16in) and 80cm (32in) length as well as a set of DPNs*

**For small circumference in the round; alternatively, use a long circular with the Magic Loop method.*

Always use needle size(s) needed to achieve tension/gauge.

Notions: Stitch markers, waste yarn, 7(7, 7, 8, 8)(8, 8, 9, 9) 25mm (1in) buttons

For reinforcing steeks, use one of the following (see Techniques for additional information):
For crocheted steeks: 3.5mm (UK 10/9, E-4) crochet hook and 4-ply (fingering) weight yarn
For machine-sewn steeks: sewing machine and thread
For hand-stitched steeks: a sewing needle and thread

TENSION/GAUGE

13 sts and 18 rounds = 10cm (4in) over st st and Colourwork Chart worked in the round using larger needle after blocking

Due to potential differences in one's tension/gauge, it is recommended that you swatch both st st and colourwork in the round; some knitters find they need to go up a needle size to achieve the same tension/gauge when working colourwork.

Note that tension/gauge is looser than often seen in these type of Aran weight garments. Once wet blocked, Icelandic yarn blooms beautifully.

PATTERN NOTES

When working this colourwork pattern, hold the pattern colour to the left of the background colour, regardless of how you hold your yarn; the float of the pattern colour should lie below the float of the background colour on the WS. For the yoke charts, MC and CC3 are background colours; the other CC colours are pattern colours.

Use the correct Yoke and Yoke Steek charts for the size you are working.

See the separate Yoke Steek and Body Trim Steek charts for the centre front steek's striping pattern. Break yarn colour(s) at the end of rounds that are not worked on the following round.

All stitch counts include steek stitches unless otherwise noted.

The German Short Row method is used to shape the lower back yoke.

See pattern for how to lengthen body and/or sleeves (note that more yarn would be required).

See Techniques for additional instructions on the following: Steeks, Long-Tail Cast-On, German Short Rows, Backwards Loop Cast-On. (Use your preferred method for securing the steek given the qualities of your particular yarn. For the listed yarn, we recommend securing the steek by machine.)

INSTRUCTIONS

YOKE

Using smaller circular needle and CC1, CO 59(63, 67, 67, 71)(75, 79, 83, 87) sts using the Long-Tail Cast-On or your preferred stretchy cast-on.

PM for BOR and join for working in the round, being careful not to twist.

Set-up Round: k3 steek sts, PM, k1, *p1, k1; rep from * to last 3 sts, PM, k3 steek sts (53(57, 61, 61, 65)(69, 73, 77, 81) sts and 6 steek sts; BOR is at centre of steek).

Rib Round 1: k3, SM, k1, *p1, k1; rep from * to marker, SM, k3.

Work rib round a total of five times or until collar measures 3.75cm (1½in) from cast-on edge.

Change to larger circular needle and knit 1 rnd.

Colourwork
Note: see BOR location for Yoke Steek Chart: for all sizes, charted yoke rounds begin with the last three sts of the Yoke Steek Chart (columns 4, 5 and 6) and end with the first three sts of the Yoke Steek Chart (columns 1, 2 and 3). The same is true when working the Body Trim Steek before working the hem. All charts are worked in st st (knit on RS).

Set-up Round: work round 1 of the Yoke Steek Chart for your size to marker, SM, work round 1 of the Yoke Chart for your size to marker, SM, complete round 1 of the Yoke Steek Chart to end.
Last rnd sets chart patterns. Joining new colours as indicated and changing to longer circular needle (same size) as needed to accommodate number of sts on needle, continue working yoke from charts until round 26(26, 26, 26, 26)(30, 30, 30, 30) is complete (163(175, 187, 187, 199)(211, 223, 235, 247) total sts).

Break all CCs.

Continue in MC, working steek sts in MC only, and knit 1 rnd.

Inc Round: k3, SM, k11(15, 23, 8, 12)(7, 14, 10, 13), M1, *k27(28, 45, 11, 7)(12, 10, 11, 12), M1; rep from * to last 11(14, 23, 8, 6)(6, 13, 10, 12) sts before marker, knit to marker, SM, k3 (169(181, 191, 203, 225)(228, 244, 255, 267) total sts).

Knit 4(4, 6, 8, 9)(5, 6, 7, 8) rnds.

Sizes 1–5
Proceed to Shape Back Yoke with German Short Rows.

Sizes 6–9
Inc Round: k3, SM, k–(–, –, –, –)(7, 14, 11, 12), M1, *k–(–, –, –, –)(13, 11, 12, 14), M1; rep from * to last –(–, –, –, –)(7, 14, 10, 11) sts, knit to marker, SM, k3 (–(–, –, –, –)(245, 265, 275, 285) total sts).
Knit –(–, –, –, –)(5, 5, 6, 7) rnds.

All Sizes
Shape Back Yoke with German Short Rows
Short Row 1 (RS): k3, SM, k119(129, 133, 141, 157)(171, 183, 189, 195), turn.
Short Row 2 (WS): DS, p74(82, 80, 84, 94)(102, 108, 108, 110), turn.
Short Row 3: DS, knit to previous DS, resolve DS, k5, turn.
Short Row 4: DS, purl to previous DS, resolve DS, p5, turn.
Short Row 5: DS, knit to BOR marker, do not turn. Resume working in the round, resolving all rem DSs as you come to them.

Knit 1 rnd.

Divide for Body and Sleeves
Note: use the Backwards Loop Cast-On when casting on sts in the next rnd.

Division Round: k3, SM, k21(23, 26, 28, 32)(34, 38, 40, 42) for left front, place next 36(38, 38, 40, 44)(48, 52, 52, 52) sts on waste yarn for left sleeve, CO 6(8, 10, 12, 12)(12, 14, 14, 16) sts for underarm, k49(53, 57, 61, 68)(75, 79, 85, 91) sts for back, place next 36 (38, 38, 40, 44)(48, 52, 52, 52) sts on waste yarn for right sleeve, CO 6(8, 10, 12, 12)(12, 14, 14, 16) sts for underarm, knit to marker, SM, k3 (103(115, 129, 141, 155)(167, 183, 193, 207) sts rem for body + 6 steek sts).

BODY

Work in st st without shaping until body measures 25cm (10in) from underarm or to 7cm (2¾in) short of desired length.

Sizes 1, 2 and 8
Proceed to All Sizes.

Sizes 3, 4, 7 and 9
Dec Round: 3, SM, k–(–, 32, 34, –)(–, 44, –, 50), k2tog, k–(–, 64, 68, –)(–, 90, –, 102), k2tog, k to marker, SM, k3 (2 sts dec; –(–, 127, 139, –)(–, 181, –, 205) sts rem + 6 steek sts).

Sizes 5 and 6
Inc Round: k3, SM, k–(–, –, –, 39)(42, –, –, –), M1, k– (–, –, –, 78)(84, –, –, –), M1, k to marker, SM, k3 (2 sts inc; –(–, –, –, 157)(169, –, –, –) sts + 6 steek sts).

All Sizes
(103(115, 127, 139, 157)(169, 181, 193, 205) sts + 6 steek sts)

BODY TRIM

Join CC1 and CC3 when indicated on chart.

Set-up Round: work round 1 of Body Trim Steek Chart to marker (beginning at BOR, columns 4–6), SM, work Body Trim Chart to marker, SM, complete round 1 of Body Trim Steek Chart to end (columns 1–3).

Work next 3 rnds of charts in established pattern until round 4 is complete.

Change to smaller circular needle and with CC1, knit 1 rnd.

Next Round: knit to marker, SM, k1, *p1, k1; rep from * to marker, SM, knit to end.

Work last round without shaping for 5cm (2in). Cast (bind) off all sts in pattern.

SLEEVES

Using larger needle(s) (DPNs or long circular if using Magic Loop), MC, and starting at centre of underarm, p&k 3(4, 5, 6, 6)(6, 7, 7, 8) underarm sts, knit across 36(38, 38, 40, 44)(48, 52, 52, 52) held sleeve sts, p&k rem 3(4, 5, 6, 6)(6, 7, 7, 8) underarm sts, PM for BOR (42 (46, 48, 52, 56) (60, 66, 66, 68) sts).

Knit 4 rnds.
Dec Round: k1, ssk, knit to last 3 sts, k2tog, k1 (2 sts dec).

Continue working in st st and repeat Dec Round every 30th(15th, 12th, 15th, 11th)(8th, 10th, 7th, 8th) rnd 2(4, 4, 3, 5)(3, 2, 2, 9) more times, then every 0(0, 12th, 16th, 10th)(8th, 5th, 6th, 0) rnd 0(0, 1, 1, 1) (5, 9, 9, 0) time(s) (36(36, 42, 42)(42, 42, 42, 48) sts rem).

Work in st st without shaping until sleeve measures 36(37.5, 38, 38, 38.5)(40, 40, 41.5, 42.5)cm/14¼(14¾, 15, 15, 15¼)(15¾, 15¾, 16¼, 16¾)in from underarm or until 7cm (2¾in) short of desired length.

SLEEVE TRIM

Join CC1 and CC3 when indicated on chart.

Work rounds 1–4 of Sleeve Trim Chart. Break MC and CC3.

Change to smaller needle(s) and CC1, knit 1 rnd.

Rib Round: *k1, p1; rep from * to end of rnd.

Work rib round for 5cm (2in).

Cast (bind) off all sts in rib pattern.

FINISHING

Secure the front steek using your preferred method and cut steek (before cutting, smooth all ends along steek towards its centre so that they are trimmed in the cutting process).

Weave in remaining ends. Block to finished measurements.

Button Band

With RS of left front edge facing, using smaller, longer circular needle, and CC1, p&k 83(83, 87, 87, 87)(91, 91, 95, 95) sts (approx. 4 sts per 2.5cm (1in); final number should be an odd number). Do not join to work in the round; button band is worked flat.

Row 1 (WS): p2, *k1, p1; rep from * to last st, p1.
Row 2 (RS): k2, *p1, k1; rep from * to last st, k1.
Work rows 1 and 2 three times total, then work row 1 one more time, ending on a WS row.

With RS facing, cast (bind) off all sts in established rib pattern.

Place markers for 7(7, 7, 8, 8)(8, 8, 9, 9) buttons evenly spaced along button band, leaving approx. 1.5–2.5cm (½–1in) between top and bottom edges from top and bottom buttons.

Buttonhole Band

With RS of right front edge facing, using smaller, longer circular needle, and CC1, p&k 83(83, 87, 87, 87)(91, 91, 95, 95) sts (matching same st count as for Button Band if your numbers vary).

Work as for Button Band, working buttonholes opposite markers on Button Band on the second time row 2 is worked (the centre row of the Buttonhole Band) by YO, work 2tog (working k2tog or p2tog to maintain established rib pattern) for each buttonhole position.

Cast (bind) off all sts in established rib pattern.

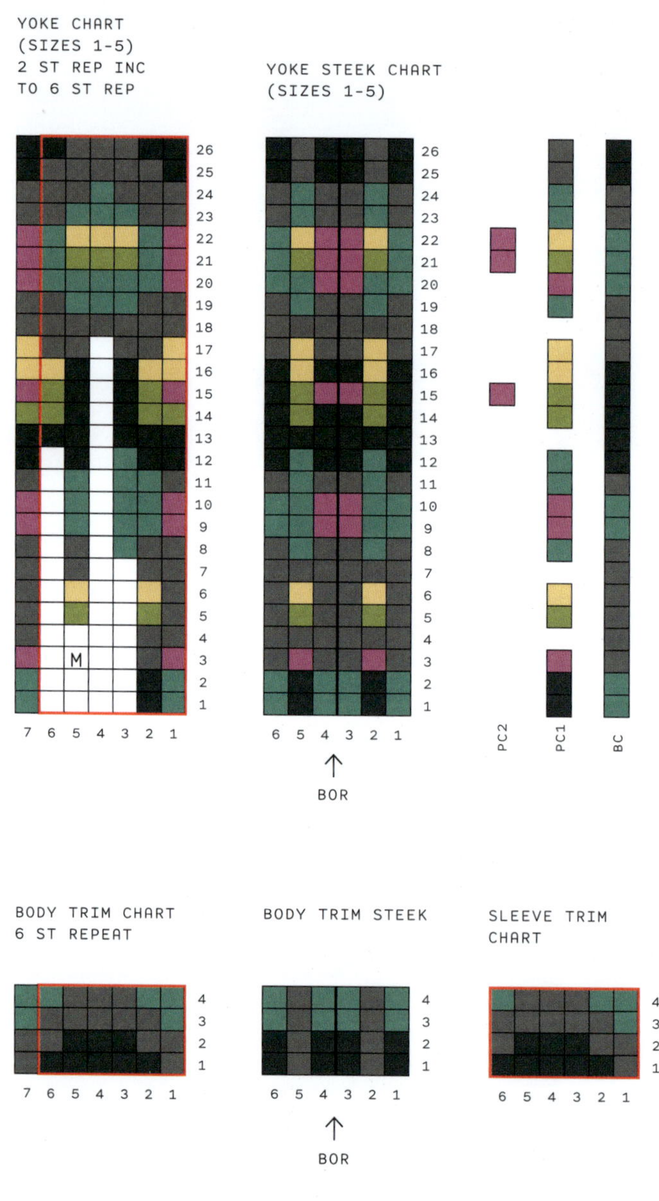
YOKE CHART
(SIZES 1-5)
2 ST REP INC
TO 6 ST REP
YOKE STEEK CHART
(SIZES 1-5)
M
BOR
PC2
PC1
BC
BODY TRIM CHART
6 ST REPEAT
BODY TRIM STEEK
SLEEVE TRIM
CHART
BOR

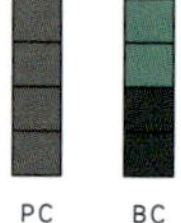
PC
BC

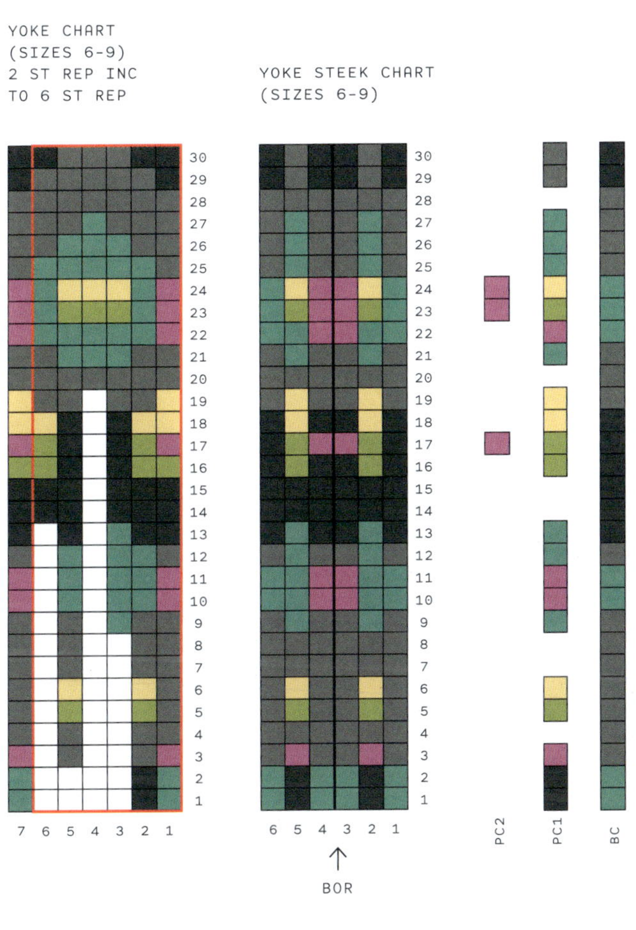

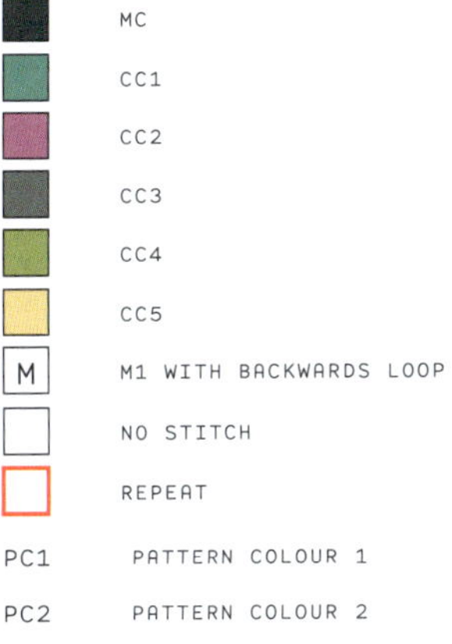

PC1 PATTERN COLOUR 1

PC2 PATTERN COLOUR 2

BC BACKGROUND COLOUR

CLIFFS AND CAKES

by Gudrun Johnston

One of the first photos of MJ and me in Shetland was taken at Eshaness, a volcanic peninsula on the west coast of mainland Shetland. It's a series of several comedic images in which MJ's hair is blowing in all directions (including across my face) while the dramatic cliffs are being pounded by the Atlantic Ocean behind us. Now – many, many silly Shetland selfies of us later – Eshaness is a place we love to introduce people to and let them experience their own version of being literally blown away!

There are lots of points of interest on the way to and from the northwest coast of mainland Shetland. We always enjoy making a full day out of it. A forest, fish and chips, a cake fridge, a giant drinking horse and signposts of descriptive-sounding and hard-to-pronounce place names steeped in Norse heritage all make up the experience of this adventure.

Once we make sure we have all the layers for all the weather possibilities, we head off from Burrastow, winding our way to Weisdale Voe (a shallow fjord-like inlet) where we take the smaller B-road connector that takes us through a very atypical Shetland landscape. For just a few seconds we are ensconced by the quiet embrace of the Kergord forest. Knitting must be put aside or you'll miss it!

Our journey continues north in the more familiar, treeless landscape, taking us past the village of Voe. A little roadside plaque tells us how the knitwear factory, T. M. Adie & Sons (now closed), produced sweaters to help keep Edmund Hillary and Tenzing Norgay warm during their Mt Everest expedition in the 1950s. Slightly less exciting but also important is to stop and use the public loos located across the road: with such an open landscape, it's hard to find things to pee behind!

We branch off the main road not long after the narrow isthmus known as Mavis Grind. This is where one can technically throw a stone from the shores of the North Sea to the Atlantic Ocean (I have never seen this done, however)! Here, you can also take a moment to imagine the Vikings heaving their boats across for a quick portage or maybe you'll get lucky and catch a glimpse of otters crossing.

When we spot Dore Holm, a little island with a natural arch that looks like a giant horse drinking from the water, we know we are near our destination. After a brief pep talk at the car park by the Eshaness lighthouse – which mostly consists of us emphasizing the need to stay well away from the edges – we set off on our circular cliff walk.

One of the wonderful things about walking in Shetland is the open access law. You can basically go wherever you want as long as you don't trample crops or leave gates open for sheep to escape. This also means there are lots of stiles to climb over. They come in many iterations and, as they can be spotted from a distance, help keep you on the right track.

After lots of practice climbing stiles, we spot the Jenga-like pile of ignimbrite blocks that have been haphazardly tossed up by the sea. The Grind O Da Navir (The Devil's Gate) is upon us. This is our turning-around point and also when we start to dream about the fish and chips (and mushy peas) that lie ahead at Frankie's in the village of Brae.

It's impossible to imagine you will fit in any more food, even if you only order the peerie fish supper, but our trip would not be complete without a stop at the infamous cake fridge which can be found on the back road between Voe and Bixter. It is literally a fridge on the side of the road filled with delectable, cakey treats. What better way to end the day!

RIGGIES CARDI

by Gudrun Johnston

'Riggies' are what the ridges in garter stitch rows are referred to in Shetland knitting. This cardigan is all about this most basic and grounding of stitches, taken a step beyond by an atypical construction. I always make sure to have this style of throw-on-and-cozy-up garment at hand for sheltering in the cottage when it's blustery outside.

CONSTRUCTION

This oversized, open-front garter stitch cardigan is worked flat in pieces from side to side. When worn, garter ridges are vertical. Short Rows are used to shape the shoulders. Stitches are picked up along the individual front and back pieces for a garter rib hem. A visible Three-Needle Cast- (Bind-) Off is used along the shoulders, centre back and side seams. Sleeve stitches are picked up and worked flat in garter stitch, ending with a garter rib cuff; sleeves are then seamed with mattress stitch. Stitches are picked up along the front body and back neck to work the neckband in garter rib which is finished with a narrow, rolled edge. Optional patch pockets finished with an I-Cord edge are worked and applied after garment completion.

SIZES

1(2, 3)

FINISHED MEASUREMENTS

Chest circumference: 124.5(146,167.5)cm/ 49(57½, 66)in
Body length: 75.5(82, 87.5)cm/29¾(32¼, 34½)in
Side length from underarm: 36(36, 35)cm/ 14¼(14¼, 13¾)in
Upper sleeve circumference: 33(37.5, 44.5)cm/ 13(14¾, 17½)in
Sleeve length from underarm: 23(23, 23)cm/ 9(9, 9)in
Cross-back width: 63(73.5, 84.5)cm/24¾(29, 33)in
Front opening width: 9(12.5, 16.5)cm/3½(5, 6½)in
Designed to be worn with 25–50cm (10–20in) of positive ease. This is a very oversized cardigan which can accommodate a wide range of body sizes. Check other measurements in size table when deciding which size to make, paying particular attention to the cross-back width. Also refer to Pattern Notes for places where size adjustments can be made. Model is wearing size 2 with 45.5cm (18in) of positive ease.

MATERIALS

Yarn: DK (8-ply/light worsted) weight yarn in the following approx. amounts: 1420(1645, 1920)m/ 1550(1800, 2100)yds

Shown in: Jamieson's of Shetland Double Knitting (100% Shetland wool; 25g/1oz/75m/82yds) in shade 429 Old Gold
19(22, 26) balls

Needles:
Ribbing: 4.5mm (UK 7, US 7) circular needle, 60cm (24in) and 100cm (40in) length
Main: 5mm (UK 6, US 8) circular needle, 80cm (32in) length
Finishing (for Three-Needle Cast- (Bind-) Off):
1 spare circular ribbing needle, 100cm (40in) length for Three-Needle Cast- (Bind-) Off at back and sides,
1 spare circular main needle, 80cm (32in) length for Three-Needle Cast- (Bind-) Off at shoulders and
1 needle one size larger than main needle

Notions: Stitch marker, waste yarn, tapestry needle

TENSION/GAUGE

17 sts and 34 rows = 10cm (4in) over garter stitch worked flat using main needle, after blocking

19 sts and 32 rows = 10cm (4in) over Garter Rib worked flat using ribbing needle, after blocking

PATTERN NOTES

It is possible to make some adjustments to the pattern to achieve your preferred fit:
The upper arm circumference can be increased or decreased by picking up more or fewer stitches from the side seams of the body. This will affect the sleeve shaping and adjustments will need to be made to the sleeve decrease rate in order to reach a desired cuff circumference.

The number of stitches cast on at the beginning of each body section determines the overall length of the cardigan, which increases with each size. It is possible to pick any one of these lengths by casting on a different number of stitches and still follow instructions for your chosen body size. This will alter the proportions of things like the side body placement when worn.

Wrap + Turn Short Rows are used to shape the shoulder pieces.

Slip all stitches purlwise unless otherwise specified.

See Techniques for additional instructions on the following: Long-Tail Cast-On, Wrap + Turn Short Rows, Three-Needle Cast- (Bind-) Off, I-Cord Cast- (Bind-) Off, mattress stitch for garter stitch.

STITCH PATTERNS

Garter stitch (worked flat)
Row 1 (RS): knit.
Row 2 (WS): knit.
Repeat rows 1 and 2 for pattern.

Garter Rib (worked flat, multiple of 4 sts)
Row 1 (WS): p1, *k2, p2; rep from * to last 3 sts, k2, p1.
Row 2 (RS): knit.
Repeat rows 1 and 2 for pattern.

INSTRUCTIONS

LEFT FRONT

Using main circular needle and the Long-Tail Cast-On, CO 115(125, 135) sts.

Next Row (WS): knit.

Before beginning the next row, mark the WS to help keep track when working in garter st. This applies to all pieces of the body.

Shape Left Front Shoulder
Next, short rows are worked to shape the shoulders; the Wrap + Turn Short Row method is used (see Techniques for additional information). A marker is used to help identify which is the wrapped st. Once you are comfortable recognizing this wrapped st, you can remove the marker if you prefer.

Short Row 1 (RS): knit to 2 sts before end of row, W+T next st.
Short Row 2 (WS): place marker on RHN after turning, knit to end of row.

Short Row 3: knit to 1 st before short row marker, sl1, remove marker, W+T the slipped st.
Short Row 4: place marker on RHN after turning, knit to end of row.
Repeat short rows 3 and 4 another 36(42, 48) times.

Break yarn leaving a tail and place the live sts onto two pieces of waste yarn as follows:
Place 39(45, 51) shoulder sts (the sloped short row section to marker) on one piece of waste yarn (removing the short row marker in the process) and then place the rem 76(80, 84) sts that were not part of the short rows onto a separate piece of waste yarn.

Left Front Hem
Using shorter circular ribbing needle and with RS facing, p&k 52(60, 68) sts along bottom edge of Left Front (pick up at a rate of approx. 2 sts out of 3 rows).

Work Garter Rib pattern 12 times (24 rows worked), ending on a RS row.

Cast (bind) off all sts in rib pattern as per Row 1 (WS) of Garter Rib.

RIGHT FRONT

Using main circular needle and the Long-Tail Cast-On, CO 115(125, 135) sts.

Shape Right Front Shoulder

Short Row 1 (WS): knit to 2 sts before end of row, W+T next st
Short Row 2 (RS): place marker on RHN after turning, knit to end of row.

Short Row 3: knit to 1 st before short row marker, sl1, remove marker, W+T the slipped st.
Short Row 4: place marker on RHN after turning, knit to end of row.
Repeat short rows 3 and 4 another 36(42, 48) times.

Next Row (WS): knit across 76(80, 84) sts.

Break yarn leaving a tail and place the live sts onto two pieces of waste yarn as follows:
Place 76(80, 84) sts just worked onto a piece of waste yarn and then place the remaining 39(45, 51) shoulder sts onto a separate piece of waste yarn (removing the short row marker in the process).

Right Front Hem

Using shorter circular ribbing needle and with RS facing, p&k 52(60, 68) sts along bottom edge of Right Front (pick up at a rate of approx. 2 sts:3 rows).
Work Garter Rib pattern 12 times (24 rows worked), ending on a RS row.

Cast (bind) off all sts in rib pattern as per Row 1 (WS) of Garter Rib.

RIGHT BACK

Using main circular needle and the Long-Tail Cast-On, CO 115(125, 135) sts.

Beginning and ending with a WS row, knit 29(35, 41) rows.

Shape Right Back Shoulder

Short Row 1 (RS): knit to 2 sts before end of row, W+T next st.
Short Row 2 (WS): place marker on RHN after turning, knit to end of row.

Short Row 3: knit to 1 st before short row marker, sl1, remove marker, W+T the slipped st.
Short Row 4: place marker on RHN after turning, knit to end of row.
Repeat short rows 3 and 4 another 36(42, 48) times.

Break yarn leaving a tail and place the live sts onto two pieces of waste yarn as follows:
Place 39(45, 51) shoulder sts (the sloped short row section to marker) on one piece of waste yarn (removing the short row marker in the process) and then place the remaining 76(80, 84) sts (that were not part of the short rows) onto a separate piece of waste yarn.

Right Back Hem

Using shorter circular ribbing needle and with RS facing, p&k 68(80, 92) sts along bottom edge of Right Back (pick up at a rate of approx. 2 sts:3 rows).

Work Garter Rib pattern 12 times (24 rows worked), ending on a RS row.

Cast (bind) off all sts in rib pattern as per Row 1 (WS) of Garter Rib.

LEFT BACK

Using main circular needle and the Long-Tail Cast-On, CO 115(125, 135) sts.

Beginning with a WS row and ending with a RS row, knit 28(34, 40) rows (this makes 14(17, 20) garter ridges when counting from the RS).

Shape Left Back Shoulder

Short Row 1 (WS): knit to 2 sts before end of row, W+T next st.

Short Row 2 (RS): place marker on RHN after turning, knit to end of row.

Short Row 3: knit to 1 st before short row marker, sl1, remove marker, W+T the slipped st.

Short Row 4: place marker on RHN after turning, knit to end of row.

Repeat short rows 3 and 4 another 36(42, 48) times.

Next Row (WS): knit across 76(80, 84) sts.

Break yarn leaving a tail. Place 76(80, 84) sts just worked onto a piece of waste yarn. Place the remaining 39(45, 51) shoulder sts onto a separate piece of waste yarn (removing the short row marker in the process).

Left Back Hem

Using shorter circular ribbing needle and with RS facing, p&k 68(80, 92) sts along bottom edge of Left Back (pick up at a rate of approx. 2 sts:3 rows).

Work Garter Rib pattern 12 times (24 rows worked), ending on a RS row.

Cast (bind) off all sts in rib pattern as per Row 1 (WS) of Garter Rib.

Before proceeding with joining the back and front, steam-block all pieces individually to finished measurements provided by size table.

JOIN BACKS AND SHOULDERS

Note: in preparation for joining the two back pieces, live sts for each will be placed on two separate ribbing (instead of main) needles. The Three-Needle Cast- (Bind-) Off will then be worked using a main needle.

Prepare Right Back for Joining

Using longer circular ribbing needle and with RS facing, p&k 115(125, 135) sts from the cast-on edge of the Right Back (pick up at a rate of 1 st:1 row) then p&k 18 sts along the ribbed hem (3 sts:4 rows) (133(143, 153) sts).

Break yarn, leaving a tail.

Prepare Left Back for Joining

Using a separate, longer circular ribbing needle and with RS facing, p&k 18 sts from the ribbed hem of the Left Back (3 sts:4 rows) and then p&k 115(125, 135) sts from the cast-on edge (1 st:1 row) (133 (143, 153) sts; make sure this is the same number of sts as for Right Back).

Do not break yarn; it will be used to join the two back pieces.

Join Backs

Using main needle and with the WS of the back pieces facing each other, work a Three-Needle Cast- (Bind-) Off across all sts. (Working the cast (bind) off with the WSs facing creates an intentionally visible seam on the RS.)

Join Shoulders

Place the live 39(45, 51) shoulder sts of the Left Front and Left Back onto two separate main circular needles. Beginning at the neck edge, join the two shoulder pieces using a Three-Needle Cast- (Bind-) Off with a needle that is one size larger than the main needle and with the WSs of the shoulders facing each other for an exposed seam. Note that it is important to not cast (bind) off too tightly along this section. With one st remaining at end of cast- (bind-) off, break yarn and draw tail through rem st.

Repeat the above to join the Right Front and Right Back shoulder sts.

SLEEVES

Note: sleeve circumference is adjustable. If a smaller or larger sleeve circumference is desired, place fewer or more (respectively) of the live side sts onto the needle during the set-up section for each sleeve (be sure the two sleeve st counts match and make a note of your new side seam st count for seaming later). You will also need to adjust the sleeve decrease rate to reach your desired cuff circumference.

Right Sleeve

Set-up Row: with RS facing and counting from where the shoulder join meets the live sts of the Right Back, place 27(31, 37) sts onto main circular needle, rejoin yarn and knit across these sts, p&k 1 st at centre of shoulder join seam, then place next 27(31, 37) sts of Right Front onto LHN and knit across these sts. Do not join to work in the round; sleeve will be worked flat to cuff (55(63, 75) sts).

Work in garter st for 13 rows (resulting in seven ridges), beginning and ending with a WS row.

Dec Row (RS): k1, ssk (modified), knit to last 3 sts, k2tog, k1 (2 sts dec).
Continue in garter st and repeat Dec Row every 14th(14th, 8th) row another 3(3, 5) times (47(55, 63) sts rem).

Continue in garter st for another 9(9, 11) rows, beginning and ending with a WS row.

Change to circular ribbing needle.

Next Row (RS): knit to last 3 sts, k2tog, k1 (1 st dec; 46(54, 62) sts rem).
Next Row (WS): p2, *k2, p2; rep from * to end of row.
Next Row (RS): knit.
Repeat last 2 rows three more times, ending on a RS row.

From WS, cast (bind) off all sts in rib pattern.

Steam-block sleeves to finished dimensions and allow to dry before seaming.

Using mattress stitch for garter stitch, seam the sleeve from cuff to underarm.

Left Sleeve

Set-up Row: with RS facing and counting from where the shoulder join meets the live sts of the Left Front, place 27(31, 37) sts onto main circular needle, rejoin yarn and knit across these sts, p&k 1 st at centre of shoulder join seam, then place next 27(31, 37) sts of Left Back onto LHN and knit across these sts (55(63, 75) sts).

Continue to work as for Right Sleeve.

JOIN SIDE SEAMS

Note: as done for joining the back pieces, ribbing needles will be used to hold the live sts of each piece (front and back) and a main needle will be used to work the Three-Needle Cast- (Bind-) Off.

Join Right Front and Right Back at Side Seam

Using a long circular ribbing needle and starting at the underarm of Right Front with RS facing, place held 49(49, 47) sts of Right Front onto needle, rejoin yarn and knit across these sts, then p&k 18 sts along Right Front hem (3 sts:4 rows). Break yarn leaving a tail.

Next, using a separate long circular ribbing needle and starting at the hem of the Right Back with RS facing, p&k 18 sts along Right Back hem (3 sts:4 rows), then place held 49(49, 47) sts of Right Back onto LHN and knit across these sts. Do not break yarn; it will be used to work the Three-Needle Cast- (Bind-) Off.

Join the two sets of live sts using a Three-Needle Cast- (Bind-) Off with WS facing (so seam is exposed) using main needle.

Repeat above to join the Left Front and Left Back at side seam.

NECKBAND

Note: if, when picking up sts for the neckband, your total st count varies slightly, adjust the st count on the next row by working k2tog decreases in the k2 sections of row 1 below (spacing decs along the row as evenly as possible) until you reach a st count that is a multiple of 4 + 2.

Using longer circular ribbing needle with RS facing and starting at the hem edge of the Right Front, p&k 18 sts along hem (3 sts:4 rows), p&k 114(124, 134) sts (1 st:1 row) along edge of Right Front to shoulder join, p&k 1 st at shoulder join, p&k 36(44, 52) sts across back neck (approx. 2 sts:3 rows), then p&k 1 st at next shoulder join, p&k 114(124, 134) sts (1 st:1 row) down Left Front, p&k 18 sts along remaining portion of hem (3 sts:4 rows) (302(330, 358) sts).

Row 1 (WS): p2, *k2, p2; rep from * to end of row.
Row 2 (RS): knit.
Repeat last 2 rows three more times, then 1 one more time (ending on a WS row).

Work in st st for 4 rows.

Cast (bind) off all sts.

POCKETS (OPTIONAL)

Patch pockets are first worked separately and then attached to the front body pieces.

Right Front Pocket
Using main circular needle and the Long-Tail Cast-On, CO 50 sts.

Begin short row shaping for Right Front Pocket:
Short Row 1 (WS): knit to 2 sts before end of row, W+T next st.
Short Row 2 (RS): place marker on RHN after turning, knit to end of row.

Short Row 3: knit to 1 st before short row marker, sl1, remove marker, W+T the slipped st.
Short Row 4: place marker on RHN after turning, knit to end of row.
Repeat short rows 3 and 4 another 27 times, ending on a RS row.

Next Row (WS): knit.

With RS facing, CO 3 sts and work an I-Cord Cast- (Bind-) Off to end of row (see Techniques; make sure to not cast (bind) off too tightly over the short row portion of the pocket).

Left Front Pocket
Using main circular needle and the Long-Tail Cast-On, CO 50 sts.

Next Row (WS): knit.

Begin short row shaping for Left Front Pocket:
Short Row 1 (RS): knit to 2 sts before end of row, W+T next st.
Short Row 2 (WS): place marker on RHN after turning, knit to end of row.

Short Row 3: knit to 1 st before short row marker, sl1, remove marker, W+T the slipped st.
Short Row 4: place marker on RHN after turning, knit to end of row.
Repeat short rows 3 and 4 another 27 times, ending on a WS row.

With RS facing, CO 3 sts and work an I-Cord Cast- (Bind-) Off to end of row (making sure to not bind off too tightly over the short row portion of the pocket).

Steam- or wet-block pockets before seaming to body. Seam pockets to front of cardigan as follows: With the WS of the pocket facing, line up the bottom edge of the pocket just above the hem and at the corner of the front band (see pocket seaming diagram; it will look like the pocket is hanging down below the hem). Matching the pocket's garter ridges to those of the body, seam using mattress stitch for garter stitch along this edge (1). Once the bottom edge is connected, flip the pocket up so that the RS of the pocket is now facing and seam the longer, straight edge of the pocket along the pick-up edge of the front band (2). Last, seam the shorter, straight side of the pocket following a garter ridge on the body (3) to align the pocket straight; the sloped section is left open.

FINISHING

Weave in ends. Although the majority of the cardigan has already been blocked, you may wish to do another steam-block along all seams.

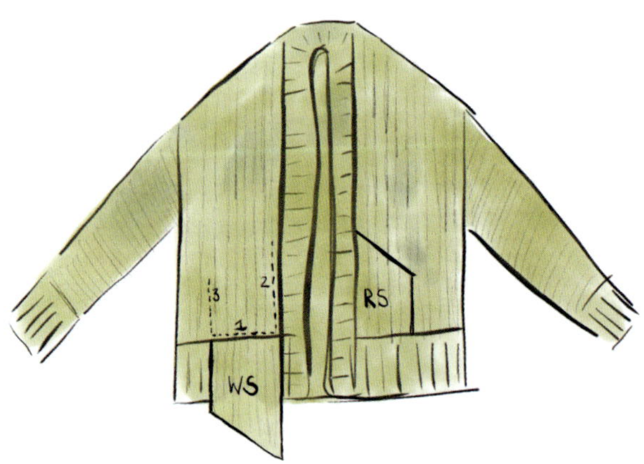

LING V-NECK SWEATER

by Mary Jane Mucklestone

One summer visit to Shetland, unaccustomed to the nearly 24-hour daylight, restless and unable to sleep, I wandered the purple heather-covered hills. At last, I lay down and dozed off. The scent of heather and sound of munching mingled in my dreams. I awoke to find a pair of Shetland ponies grazing so close I could feel their breath. New friends! Ling is the variety of heather the ponies were breakfasting on.

CONSTRUCTION

This sweater is knitted in one piece from the top down. The yoke is worked flat to the base of V-neck. Increases occur on each side of four raglan columns that demarcate the sleeves from the fronts and back. At the same time, stitches are increased at the front neck to shape the V-neck. When shoulder and neck shaping are complete, sleeve stitches are put on hold and the piece is joined for working in the round, continuing the body down through a split hem worked in 1×1 rib with selvedge/selvage edges. Sleeves are worked in the round to the ribbed cuffs. Finally, stitches are picked up around the V-neckline for working a Fair Isle neckband. Body and sleeve lengths are easily adjusted (note that any length adjustments will affect total yarn quantity required).

SIZES

1(2, 3, 4, 5)(6, 7, 8, 9)

FINISHED MEASUREMENTS

Chest circumference: 86.5(96.5, 107.5, 115.5, 125.5)(137, 146.5, 155.5, 162)cm/34(38, 42¼, 45½, 49½)(54, 57¾, 61¼, 63¾)in

Back neck width: 18.5(19.5, 19.5, 20.5, 22.5)(23.5, 25, 27.5, 27.5)cm/7¼(7¼, 7¾, 8¼, 8¾)(9¼, 9¾, 10¾, 10¾)in

Total yoke depth (without trim): 19(20.5, 23, 23.5, 24.5)(27, 28.5, 29.5, 31)cm/8¼(8½, 9½, 9¾, 10¼)(11¼, 11¾, 12½, 13)in

Side length from underarm: 34.5(34.5, 34.5, 34.5, 34.5)(34.5, 34.5, 34.5, 34.5)cm/13½(13½, 13½, 13½, 13½)(13½, 13½, 13½, 13½)in

Sleeve length from underarm: 43(43, 43, 43, 43)(43, 43, 43, 43)cm/17(17, 17, 17, 17)(17, 17, 17, 17)in

Body length: 55(56, 58.5, 59, 60.5)(63, 64, 66, 67.5)cm/21¾(22, 23, 23¼, 23¾)(24¾, 25¼, 26, 26½)in

Upper sleeve circumference: 32(33.5, 37.5, 40, 42.5)(46.5, 50, 52.5, 56)cm/12½(13¼, 14¾, 15¾, 16¾)(18¼, 19¾, 20¾, 22)in

Cuff circumference: 22(22, 24, 25, 26)(27.5, 28.5, 30, 30)cm/8¾(8¾, 9½, 9¾, 10¼)(10¾, 11¼, 11¾, 11¾)in

Designed to be worn with approx. 5–10cm (2–4in) of positive ease. Model is wearing size 2 with 7.5cm (3in) of positive ease.

MATERIALS

Yarn: 4-ply (fingering) weight yarn in the following approx. amounts:
MC: 650(725, 795, 850, 920)(1005, 1080, 1145, 1195)m/710(795, 870, 930, 1005)(1100, 1180, 1250, 1310)yds
CC1: 6(7, 8, 9, 9)(10, 11, 12, 13)m/7(8, 9, 10, 10)(11, 12, 13, 14)yds
CC2: 10(11, 12, 13, 14)(15, 16, 17, 18)m/11(12, 13, 14, 15)(16, 18, 19, 20)yds
CC3: 6(7, 8, 9, 9)(10, 11, 12, 13)m/7(8, 9, 10, 10)(11, 12, 13, 14)yds
CC4: 4(4, 5, 5, 5)(5, 5, 6, 6)m/4(4, 5, 5, 5)(6, 6, 7, 7)yds

Shown in: Jamieson's of Shetland Spindrift (100% pure Shetland wool; 25g/1oz/105m/115yds) in shades 273 Foxglove (MC), 517 Mantilla (CC1), 293 Port Wine (CC2), 794 Eucalyptus (CC3) and 135 Surf (CC4)
MC: 7(8, 9, 9, 10)(11, 12, 12, 13) balls
CC1: 1(1, 1, 1, 1)(1, 1, 1, 1) ball
CC2: 1(1, 1, 1, 1)(1, 1, 1, 1) ball
CC3: 1(1, 1, 1, 1)(1, 1, 1, 1) ball
CC4: 1(1, 1, 1, 1)(1, 1, 1, 1) ball

Needles:
Smaller (for Neckband, Hem and Cuffs): 2.75mm (UK 12, US 2) circular needle, 40cm (16in) and 60cm (24in) length* as well as a set of DPNs*
Larger (for Body and Sleeves): 3.25mm (UK 10, US 3) circular needle, 40cm (16in) length or set of DPNs* as well as 60cm (24in) or 80cm (32in) length

**For small circumference in the round; alternatively, use a long circular for Magic Loop.*

Notions: 8 stitch markers of different colours, waste yarn or stitch holders, 1 locking marker or safety pin, tapestry needle, T-pins for blocking

Notions: 8 stitch markers of different colours, waste yarn or stitch holders, 1 locking marker or safety pin, tapestry needle, T-pins for blocking

TENSION/GAUGE

24 sts and 33 rows/rounds = 10cm (4in) over Stocking (Stockinette) Stitch worked both flat and in the round on larger needle, after blocking

24 sts and 32 rounds = 10cm (4in) over Fair Isle Pattern worked in the round on smaller needle, after blocking

PATTERN NOTE

See Techniques for additional instructions on the following: Backwards Loop Cast-On.

INSTRUCTIONS

YOKE

Using larger circular needle and MC, CO 62(64, 65, 67, 75)(78, 81, 91, 91) sts. Do not join to work in the round; yoke is worked flat.

Place raglan markers as follows:
Set-up Row (WS): p2(2, 2, 2, 4)(4, 4, 4, 4) right front sts, PM, p1 raglan st, PM, p6(6, 6, 6, 6)(6, 6, 8, 8) right shoulder sts, PM, p1 raglan st, PM, p42(44, 45, 47, 51)(54, 57, 63, 63) back neck sts, PM, p1 raglan st, PM, p6(6, 6, 6, 6)(6, 6, 8, 8) left shoulder sts, PM, p1 raglan st, PM, p2(2, 2, 2, 4)(4, 4, 4, 4) left front sts.
Note: increases are worked on either side of each raglan st (indicated by markers) to shape the yoke every RS row; at the same time, increases are worked at each neck edge to shape the V-neck every other RS row. All WS rows are purled.

Inc Row 1 (RS): *knit to marker, M1R, SM, k1, SM, M1L; rep from * three more times, knit to end of row (8 sts inc).
Next Row (WS): purl.
Inc Row 2: k1, M1R, *knit to marker, M1R, SM, k1, SM, M1L; rep from * three more times, knit to last st, M1L, k1 (10 sts inc).
Next Row: purl.
Work the last 4 rows a total of 12(14, 17, 17, 17)(18, 19, 19, 20) times, ending on a WS row (278(316, 371, 373, 381)(402, 423, 433, 451) total sts: 54(62, 74, 74, 74)(78, 82, 84, 88) sts each shoulder, 38 (44, 53, 53, 55)(58, 61, 61, 64) sts each front, 90 (100, 113, 115, 119)(126, 133, 139, 143) back sts, 4 raglan sts).

Sizes 1, 2 and 3
Increase at the fronts and shoulders only (omitting increases at back raglan markers) as follows:
Inc Row 1 (RS): knit to marker, M1R, SM, k1, SM, M1L, knit to marker, M1R, SM, k1, SM, knit to marker, SM, k1, SM, M1L, knit to marker, M1R, SM, k1, SM, M1L, knit to end of row (6 sts inc).
Next Row (WS): purl.
Work the last 2 rows a total of 6(3, 2, –, –)(–, –, –, –) times, ending on a WS row.
(314(334, 383, –, –)(–, –, –, –) total sts: 44(47, 55, –, –)(–, –, –, –) sts each front and 66(68, 78, –, –)(–, –, –, –) sts each shoulder; back and raglan sts rem the same).

Increase at the neck and fronts only as follows:
Inc Row 2 (RS): k1, M1R, knit to marker, M1R, *SM, k1, SM, knit to marker; rep from * three more times, SM, M1L, knit to last st, M1L, k1 (4 sts inc; 318(338, 387, –, –)(–, –, –, –) total sts: 46(49, 57, –, –)(–, –, –, –) sts each front; back, shoulder and raglan sts rem the same).
Next Row (WS): purl.

Sizes 1 and 3
Proceed to All Sizes.

Sizes 2, 4, 5, 6, 7, 8 and 9

Inc Row 1 (RS): k1, M1R, *knit to marker, (M1R, SM, k1, SM, M1L); rep from * three more times, knit to last st, M1L, k1 (10 sts inc).

Next Row (WS): Purl.

Work the last 2 rows a total of –(1, –, 4, 6)(8, 8, 10, 10) time(s), ending on a WS row.

(–(348, –, 413, 441)(482, 503, 533, 551) total sts: –(51, –, 61, 67)(74, 77, 81, 84) sts each front, –(70, –, 82, 86)(94, 98, 104, 108) sts each shoulder, –(102, –, 123, 131)(142, 149, 159, 163) back sts and 4 raglan sts).

All Sizes: Divide for Body and Sleeves

Note: on the next row, the raglan sts are incorporated into the front and back sections. Use the Backwards Loop Cast-On when casting on sts in the next row.

Next Row (RS): knit to marker, RM, k1, RM, place next 66(70, 78, 82, 86)(94, 98, 104, 108) sts on waste yarn for left sleeve, CO 4(5, 5, 6, 7)(7, 10, 10, 12) sts for left underarm, PM for BOR, CO another 5(5, 6, 6, 7)(8, 10, 11, 12) sts for left underarm, RM, k1, RM, knit across back sts to marker, RM, k1, RM, place next 66(70, 78, 82, 86)(94, 98, 104, 108) sts on waste yarn for right sleeve, CO 4(5, 5, 6, 7)(7, 10, 10, 12) sts for right underarm, PM for side marker, CO another 5(5, 6, 6, 7)(8, 10, 11, 12) sts for right underarm, RM, k1, RM, knit to end of right front, join to work in the round, knit to BOR (204(228, 253, 273, 297)(324, 347, 367, 383) body sts).

Note: for all sizes except size 2, front and back stitch counts will vary slightly; this is intentional in order to achieve fit goals through the raglan yoke. The discrepancy will be negligible after blocking. During blocking, match raglan lines and flatten front and back to equal widths.

BOR is now at left underarm. Piece is now worked in the round to the split hem.

BODY

Work in st st in the round without shaping until work measures 26.5cm (10½in) from underarm or until 7.5cm (3in) short of desired length. On the last rnd, work the following decrease round for your size:

Sizes 1, 2 and 6

Dec Round: k2tog, knit to marker, SM, k2tog, knit to end of rnd (2 sts dec; 202(226, –, –, –)(322, –, –, –) sts rem).

Sizes 3, 4 and 5

Dec Round: k2tog, knit to 3 sts before marker, ssk, k1, SM, k2tog, knit to end of rnd (3 sts dec; –(–, 250, 270, 294)(–, –, –, –) sts rem).

Sizes 7, 8 and 9

Dec Round: k2tog, knit to end of rnd (1 st dec; –(–, –, –, –)(–, 346, 366, 382) sts rem).

SPLIT HEM

You will now work flat across the back hem sts while the front hem sts are placed on hold. Change to smaller circular needle.

Set-up Row (WS): turn work, RM (BOR), sl1 tbl wyif, *p1, k1; rep from * to 2 sts before side marker, p2, RM (101(113, 125, 135, 147)(161, 173, 183, 191) sts each for back and front).

Place front sts on hold.

Work Back Hem

Row 1 (RS): sl1 kwise, *k1, p1; rep from * to last 2 sts, k2.

Row 2 (WS): sl1 tbl wyif, *p1, k1; rep from * to last 2 sts, p2.

Work rows 1 and 2 for 7.5cm (3in), ending on a WS row. Cast (bind) off all sts in rib pattern.

Work Front Hem
Return the front sts to smaller circular needle and join MC, ready to work a WS row. Beginning with row 2 (WS), work rows 1 and 2 as for back hem, ending on a WS row. Cast (bind) off all sts in rib pattern.

SLEEVES

Note: change to shorter-length circular needle or DPNs as needed.

Return 66(70, 78, 82, 86)(94, 98, 104, 108) sleeve sts to larger needle for working small circumference in the round.

Set-up Round (RS): with MC, starting at centre of underarm sts, p&k 4(5, 5, 6, 7)(7, 10, 10, 12) sts, knit across sleeve sts, p&k rem 5(5, 6, 6, 7)(8, 10, 11, 12) sts from underarm, PM for BOR and join to work in the round (75(80, 89, 94, 100)(109, 118, 125, 132) sts).

Work in st st until sleeve measures 4cm (1½in) from underarm.

Dec Round: k1, k2tog, knit to last 3 sts, ssk, k1 (2 sts dec).

Continue working in st st and repeat Dec Round every 9th(7th, 6th, 5th, 5th)(4th, 4th, 3rd, 3rd) rnd a total of 11(14, 16, 18, 19)(22, 25, 27, 31) times (22(28, 32, 36, 38)(44, 50, 54, 62) sts dec; 53(52, 57, 58, 62)(65, 68, 71, 70) sts rem).

Continue working in st st without shaping until sleeve measures 35cm (14in) from underarm or until 7.5cm (3in) short of desired length (for cuff ribbing).

Sizes 2, 4, 5, 7 and 9
Proceed to Cuff.

Sizes 1, 3, 6 and 8
Dec Round: k1, k2tog, knit to end of rnd (1 st dec; 52(–, 56, –, –)(64, –, 70, –) sts rem).

Cuff
Change to smaller needle(s).

Rib Round: *k1, p1; rep from * to end of rnd.
Work rib round for 7.5cm (3in). Cast (bind) off all sts in rib pattern.

Repeat for second sleeve.

NECKBAND

Note: pick up sts between the edge st and the st next to it. A removable locking marker is placed on the centre st; as you work the neckband's double decreases, reposition the locking marker onto the new centre st. Use smaller diameter circular needle.

With MC, on RS and beginning at left edge of left shoulder, p&k 49(49, 61, 61, 61)(67, 67, 73, 73) sts along the left side of front neck, p&k 1 st for centre front, place locking marker on centre st, p&k 49(49, 61, 61, 61)(67, 67, 73, 73) sts along right front neck, p&k 6 sts for right shoulder, p&k 45(45, 45, 45, 45)(57, 57, 57, 57) sts for back neck, then p&k 6 sts for left shoulder (156(156, 180, 180, 180)(204, 204, 216, 216) sts).
PM for BOR and join for working in the round.

With CC1, knit to 1 st before centre st with locking marker, sl1, k2tog, psso, reposition locking marker onto new centre st, knit to end of rnd (2 sts dec; 156(156, 180, 180, 180)(204, 204, 216, 216) sts).

Note: when working Fair Isle pattern, hold the pattern colours to the left of the background colours, regardless of how you hold your yarn; the float of the pattern colour should lie below the float of the background colour. Chart guide indicates pattern and background colours. Change to shorter-length needle as needed.

Beginning where indicated for your size, work 15 rounds of Fair Isle Chart, decreasing at the centre st as indicated in the chart (128(128, 152, 152, 152)(176, 176, 188, 188) sts rem).

Break all CC yarns.

Rib Dec Round: with MC, *p1, k1; rep from * to 2 sts before centre st with locking marker, p1, CDD, reposition locking marker onto new centre st, *p1, k1; rep from * to end of rnd (2 sts dec).
Work Rib Dec Round one more time (124(124, 148, 148, 148)(172, 172, 184, 184) sts).

Cast (bind) off all sts loosely in rib pattern.

FINISHING

Weave in ends on WS. Wet-block to size, taking care to shape neckline neatly.

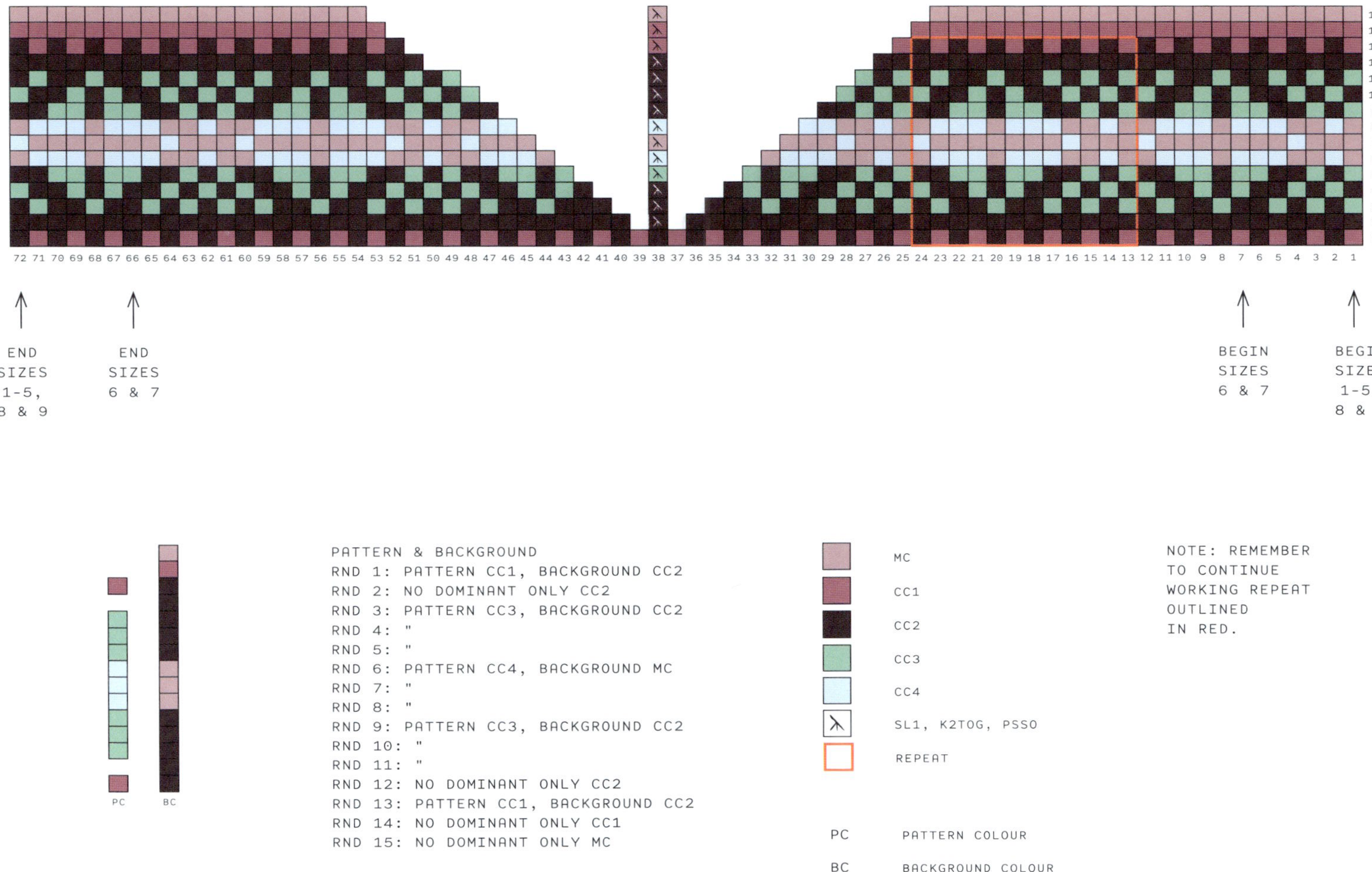
15
14
13
12
11
10
9
8
7
6
5
4
3
2
1
72 71 70 69 68 67 66 65 64 63 62 61 60 59 58 57 56 55 54 53 52 51 50 49 48 47 46 45 44 43 42 41 40 39 38 37 36 35 34 33 32 31 30 29 28 27 26 25 24 23 22 21 20 19 18 17 16 15 14 13 12 11 10 9 8 7 6 5 4 3 2 1
END SIZES 1-5, 8 & 9
END SIZES 6 & 7
BEGIN SIZES 6 & 7
BEGIN SIZES 1-5, 8 & 9
PC
BC
PATTERN & BACKGROUND
RND 1: PATTERN CC1, BACKGROUND CC2
RND 2: NO DOMINANT ONLY CC2
RND 3: PATTERN CC3, BACKGROUND CC2
RND 4: "
RND 5: "
RND 6: PATTERN CC4, BACKGROUND MC
RND 7: "
RND 8: "
RND 9: PATTERN CC3, BACKGROUND CC2
RND 10: "
RND 11: "
RND 12: NO DOMINANT ONLY CC2
RND 13: PATTERN CC1, BACKGROUND CC2
RND 14: NO DOMINANT ONLY CC1
RND 15: NO DOMINANT ONLY MC
MC
CC1
CC2
CC3
CC4
SL1, K2TOG, PSSO
REPEAT
PC PATTERN COLOUR
BC BACKGROUND COLOUR
NOTE: REMEMBER TO CONTINUE WORKING REPEAT OUTLINED IN RED.

FLOOERS COWL

by Gudrun Johnston

I'm a huge cowl advocate – I wear them all the time. For this cowl I chose to use an all-over pattern with fairly subtle contrast, a gentle reminder of the beautiful specks of colour to be found from the wildflowers dotting the hillside in the summer months. I rely on Mary Jane to fill me in on the botanical details, as she has become quite the wildflower expert over our many visits to Shetland!

CONSTRUCTION

This colourwork cowl is worked in the round from a chart beginning with a Provisional Cast-on. The live stitches from both ends are then grafted together, resulting in a double-layered fabric. When worn, the graft can be tucked away towards the inside of the cowl. See Pattern Notes for how to adjust length and/or width.

SIZE

One size

FINISHED MEASUREMENTS

Height: 21cm (8¼in)
Circumference: 59cm (23¼in)

MATERIALS

Yarn: 1–3-ply (lace) weight yarn held double in the following approx. amounts:
MC: 505m (550yds)
CC: 410m (450yds)

Shown in: La Bien Aimée Helix (75% Falkland merino, 25% Gotland wool; 100g/3½oz/650m/710yds) in shades Clay (MC) and Fluoro Morganite (CC)
MC, CC: 1 skein each

Needles:
Main: 3.5mm (UK 10/9, US 4) circular needle, 40cm (16in) length
Finishing (for Three-Needle Cast- (Bind-) Off*):* 1 spare circular main needle, 40cm (16in) length and 1 needle one size larger than main needle

Notions: stitch marker, 4-ply (fingering) weight smooth waste yarn and 3.5mm (UK 10/9, US E-4) (or same size as main needle) for the Crochet Provisional Cast-On, tapestry needle

TENSION/GAUGE

29 sts and 29 rounds = 10cm (4in) over Fair Isle Pattern with yarns held double worked in the round using main needle, after blocking

PATTERN NOTES

When working this Fair Isle pattern, hold the CC to the left of the other colour, regardless of how you hold your yarn. The float of the CC yarn should lie below the float of the MC yarn on the WS.

The cowl's size may be easily adapted by working more repeats of the stitch pattern to add width and/or length (more yarn required).

See Techniques for additional instructions on the Crochet Provisional Cast-On and Three-Needle Cast- (Bind-) Off.

INSTRUCTIONS

COWL

Using waste yarn, main needle and the Crochet Provisional Cast-On, CO 168 sts.

PM for BOR and join for working in the round, being careful not to twist.

Change to MC yarn. Holding 2 strands of MC together, knit 1 rnd.

Joining CC as directed and holding each yarn double throughout:
Next Round: work across 14 sts from round 1 of Fair Isle Chart to end of rnd.
Last rnd sets chart pattern. Continue to work from chart until rounds 1–30 have been worked a total of four times.

Knit 1 rnd in MC (leave CC attached).

Break all working yarns, leaving a long tail of CC yarn for working a Three-Needle Cast- (Bind-) Off (approx. 3m/3yds). Leave sts on needle.

FINISHING

Turn cowl inside out and weave in any ends on the WS. Turn cowl back to RS.

Undo the Provisional Cast-on and place these sts onto the spare circular main needle.

Keeping WSs together, bring one end of the cowl up the inside to meet the other end, forming two concentric rings of sts on needles. Join the two ends of the cowl using a Three-Needle Cast- (Bind-) Off with the spare larger needle. The seam will be exposed on the RS of the work; it can be adjusted towards the inside of the cowl when worn.

Soak cowl in cool water and a gentle wool wash (optional) for at least 20 minutes. Remove excess water from fabric by carefully squeezing (not wringing) and then press cowl between towels. Block to finished measurements.

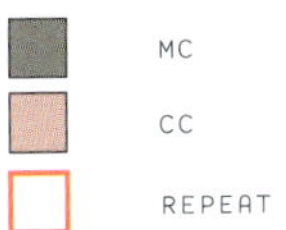

SWATCHTASTIC FLOWER HAT

by Mary Jane Mucklestone

I consider my swatches trophies, representations of time well spent. For those who avoid swatching, I say trick yourself and make this hat – you can swatch for colour and tension (gauge) all in one go! The inspiration for this hat came when I was practising stocking (stockinette) stitch tension for the Ling sweater on an unfinished hat. By the way: any other motif from my patterns in this book will fit in this hat. Go for it and have fun!

CONSTRUCTION

This hat is worked bottom up from ribbed brim through charted Fair Isle pattern followed by a solid-colour stocking (stockinette) stitch top, softly gathered with rapid crown decrease. It is finished with a jaunty, though optional pom-pom.

SIZE

One size

FINISHED MEASUREMENTS

Circumference at brim: 45.5cm (18in)
Circumference at widest point: 54cm (21½in)
Length from brim to crown as worn: 23cm (9in)

Fits head circumferences 48–53cm (19–21in) with 2.5–7.5cm (1–3in) of negative ease.

MATERIALS

Yarn: 4-ply (fingering) weight yarn in the following approx. amounts:
MC: 110m (120yds)
CC1: 15m (15yds)
CC2: 20m (20yds)
CC3: 10m (10yds)
CC4: 20m (20yds)
CC5: 10m (10yds)
CC6: 5m (5yds)
Approx. additional 35m (40yds) total in chosen colour(s) for optional pom-pom.

Shown in: Jamieson & Smith 2-ply Jumper Weight (100% Shetland wool; 25g/1oz/115m/125yds) in shades 118 Medium Green (MC), FC11 Bright Grass Green (CC1), 65 Marled Mid Green (CC2), 125 Orange (CC3), 142 Dark Azure Blue (CC4), 93 Bright Red (CC5) and 132 Azure Blue (CC6)
MC, CC1, CC2, CC3, CC4, CC5 and CC6:
1 ball each

Needles:
Ribbing: 2.75mm (UK 12, US 2) circular needle, 40cm (16in) length*
Main: 3.25mm (UK 10, US 3) circular needle, 40cm (16in) length* and a set of DPNs*

**For small circumference in the round; alternatively, use a long circular with the Magic Loop method.*

Notions: 1 stitch marker, tapestry needle, pom-pom maker (optional)

TENSION/GAUGE

27 sts and 30 rounds = 10cm (4in) over Fair Isle Pattern worked in the round using main needle, after blocking

PATTERN NOTE

Regardless of how you hold your yarn when working stranded colourwork, hold the pattern colour to the left of the background colour; the float of the pattern colour should lie below the float of the background colour on the WS.

INSTRUCTIONS

BRIM

Using ribbing needle and MC, CO 128 sts using your preferred stretchy cast-on.

PM for BOR and join for working in the round, being careful not to twist.

Rib Round: *k2, p2; rep from * to end of rnd.
Work rib round a total of 13 times or until ribbing measures 3.25cm (1¼in) from cast on edge.

Inc Round: *work in rib pattern for 8 sts, M1L; rep from * to end of rnd (16 sts inc; 144 sts).

BODY

Change to main circular needle and knit 1 rnd with MC.

Next Round: work across 24 sts from round 1 of Fair Isle Chart to end of rnd.
Last rnd sets chart pattern. Continue to work from chart as set, joining CCs as indicated, until round 25 is complete. Break all yarns except MC.

With MC work in st st for 9cm (3½in) or to desired length before beginning crown decreases (crown adds approx. 3cm (1¼in) to total length).

CROWN

Note: change to main DPNs as needed while working crown.

Dec Round 1: *k2tog; rep from * to end of rnd (72 sts dec; 72 sts rem).
Knit 2 rnds.
Dec Round 2: *k2tog; rep from * to end of rnd (36 sts dec; 36 sts rem).
Knit 2 rnds.
Dec Round 3: *k2tog; rep from * to end of rnd (18 sts dec; 18 sts rem).
Knit 1 rnd.
Dec Round 4: *k2tog; rep from * to end of rnd (9 sts dec; 9 sts rem).
Knit 1 rnd.

FINISHING

Break yarn and thread tail through rem sts. Secure to the inside of the hat. Weave in ends. Wet block. Lay flat or shape atop an inflated balloon and leave to dry.

For optional pom-pom, make a 5cm (2in) pom-pom with CC3 or your favourite colour(s). Secure to the top of the hat when dry for extra pizzazz!

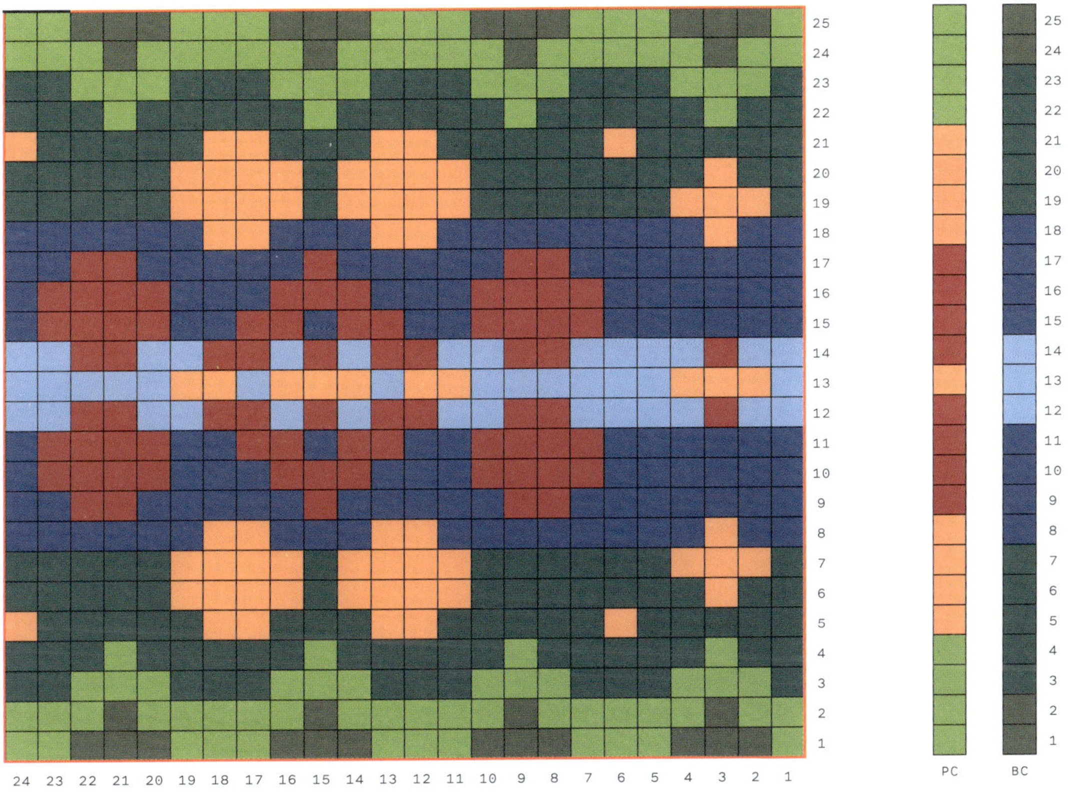

MC

CC1

CC2

CC3

CC4

CC5

CC6

REPEAT

PC PATTERN COLOUR

BC BACKGROUND COLOUR

SNOW TREASURE GLOVES

by Mary Jane Mucklestone

Gloves are wonderful souvenirs from Shetland; each pair is a treasure of colour and design. And practical – I always need them, even in summer. This set reflects Shetland's Nordic connection, combining Scandinavian-style stars with Shetland shading. The design is inspired by a children's book that parallels the story of Shetland's involvement in the WW2 Norwegian resistance, where naval boats left Shetland disguised as working fishing boats, just like in the story.

CONSTRUCTION

These gloves are worked in the round from corrugated ribbed cuff through the charted colourwork hand, featuring a star pattern on the back of the hand and a zigzag patterned palm. Fingers are worked individually, long for gloves, or finished with 1×1 rib for the fingerless pair. Both versions have an afterthought thumb.

SIZE

One size

FINISHED MEASUREMENTS

Palm circumference: 20cm (7¾in)
Wrist circumference: 17.75cm (7in)
Length (glove version, from cuff to fingertips): 26.5cm (10.5in)
Length (fingerless version): 20.25cm (8in)

MATERIALS

Yarn: 4-ply (fingering) weight yarn in the following approx. amounts for gloves (for fingerless version, deduct approx. 20m (25yds) of MC):
MC: 135m (150yds)
CC1: 45m (50yds)
CC2: 18m (20yds)
CC3: 10m (10yds)

Shown in: Rauma Finull PT2 (100% Norwegian wool; 50g/1¾oz/175m/190yds) in shades 424 Red (MC), 451 Light Peasant Blue (CC1), 472 Sky Blue (CC2) and 4406 Light Blue (CC3)
MC, CC1, CC2 and CC3: 1 ball each

Needles:
Smaller (for Ribbing, Fingers and Thumbs): 2.25mm (UK 13, US 1) set of DPNs*
Larger (for Charted Colourwork): 2.75mm (UK 12, US 2) set of DPNs*
**For small circumference in the round; alternatively, use a long circular with the Magic Loop method.*

Notions: Stitch markers (including 1 locking stitch marker or safety pin), 4-ply (fingering) weight smooth waste yarn in a contrasting colour, tapestry needle

TENSION/GAUGE

32 sts and 32 rounds = 10cm (4in) over Fair Isle Pattern on larger needle, after blocking

34 sts and 36 rounds = 10cm (4in) over corrugated ribbing on smaller needle, after blocking

PATTERN NOTES

Regardless of how you hold your yarn when working stranded colourwork, hold the pattern colour (CC1–CC3) to the left of the background colour (MC); the float of the pattern colour should lie below the float of the background colour on the WS.

See Techniques for additional information on Afterthought Thumbs and the Backwards Loop Cast-On.

Refer to instructions at the end of the pattern if you prefer to work fingerless gloves rather than long-fingered gloves (see page 150).

The fingerless version can be seen in the photo on page 136.

INSTRUCTIONS

CUFF

With smaller needle(s) and MC, CO 60 sts using your preferred stretchy cast-on. Divide sts evenly onto 3 DPNs (or on a longer circular needle for Magic Loop). PM for BOR and join for working in the round, being careful not to twist.

Work 23 rounds of corrugated ribbing while changing CC colours as follows:
Rounds 1–7: *k1 with MC, p1 with CC1; rep from * to end of rnd.
Rounds 8–11: *k1 with MC, p1 with CC2; rep from * to end of rnd.
Round 12: *k1 with MC, p1 with CC3; rep from * to end of rnd.
Rounds 13–16: repeat Rounds 8–11.
Rounds 17–23: repeat Rounds 1–7.

Inc Round: with MC only, k1, M1L, k30, M1L, knit to end of rnd (2 sts inc; 62 sts).

Change to larger needle(s). Redistribute sts with half (31 sts) for back of hand (BOH) and the other half (31 sts) for palm (if using DPNs, place BOH sts on one needle and divide palm sts across two needles).

HAND

Next Round: Work across 62 sts from round 1 of Fair Isle Chart to end of rnd.
Changing colours as indicated, continue to work from chart through round 16.

Thumb Set-up: Right Hand Only
Round 17: work 33 sts from chart; with waste yarn, k10; break waste yarn; slip 10 sts just worked back to LHN pwise; resume working from chart to end of rnd.

Thumb Set-up: Left Hand Only
Round 17: work 50 sts from chart; with waste yarn, k10; break waste yarn; slip 10 sts just worked back to LHN pwise; resume working from chart to end of rnd.

There are now 10 sts of waste yarn in the fabric. After finishing the glove, you will return to these sts, unpick the waste yarn and work an afterthought thumb.

Continue to work from chart up to and including round 36.

Break all CC, leaving MC attached.

FINGERS (GLOVE VERSION ONLY)

Fingers and thumb are worked on smaller needle(s). Use the Backwards Loop Cast-On when casting on new sts.

Keeping BOR marker in place and maintaining an even split between sts for BOH and palm, slip 31 sts for each side onto a spare needle or stitch holder.

Little Finger
Beginning at side of work furthest from thumb, sl 7 sts from each side (BOH and palm) onto smaller needle(s).

Set-up Round: with MC and starting at (palm for L hand, BOH for R hand), k7, CO 2 sts, k7 (16 sts).

Work in st st (knit every rnd) until finger measures 4.5cm (1¾in) or 1.25cm (½in) less than desired length.

Dec Round: *k2tog, k2; rep from * to end of rnd (12 sts).
Next Round: knit.
Final Dec Round: *k2tog; rep from * to end of rnd (6 sts).

Break yarn. Thread tail through rem sts and fasten off.

Ring Finger
Sl next 8 sts from each side (BOH and palm) adjacent to Little Finger onto smaller needle(s).

Set-up Round: with MC and starting at palm, k8, CO 1 st, k8, p&k 1 st from base of Little Finger (18 sts).

Work in st st until finger measures 5cm (2in) or 1.25cm (½in) less than desired length.

Dec Round 1: *k2tog, k7; rep from * to end of rnd (16 sts).
Next Round: knit.
Dec Round 2: *k2tog, k2; rep from * to end of rnd (12 sts).
Next Round: knit.
Final Dec Round: *k2tog; rep from * to end of rnd (6 sts).

Break yarn. Thread tail through rem sts and fasten off.

Middle Finger
Sl next 8 sts from each side (BOH and palm) adjacent to Ring Finger and work as for Ring Finger until finger measures 6.5cm (2½in) or 1.25cm (½in) less than desired length. Decrease as set.

Break yarn. Thread tail through rem sts and fasten off.

INDEX FINGER

Sl next 8 sts from each side (BOH and palm) adjacent to Middle Finger onto smaller needle(s).

Set-up Round: with MC and starting at (palm for L hand, BOH for R hand), k16, p&k 2 sts from the base of the Middle Finger (18 sts).

Work in st st until finger measures 5cm (2in) or 1.25cm (½in) less than desired length.

Dec Round 1: *k2tog, k7; rep from * to end of rnd (16 sts).
Next Round: knit.
Dec Round 2: *k2tog, k2; rep from * to end of rnd (12 sts).
Next Round: knit.
Final Dec Round: *k2tog; rep from * to end of rnd (6 sts).

THUMB (BOTH VERSIONS)

Using smaller needle(s), pick up the right leg of each of the 10 sts directly below the waste yarn sts. Then using a second (same size) needle, pick up the right leg of each of the 10 sts directly above the waste yarn sts. Carefully remove the waste yarn, making sure that all sts are safely on needles (20 sts).

Distribute sts equally across needle(s).

Set-up Round: with MC, knit 1 rnd AND at the same time p&k 1 st in the two opposite corners of the thumb opening (note that you may need to hold CC sts in place as you knit them on the first rnd) (22 sts).

Work in st st until thumb measures 4.5cm (1¾in) or 1.25cm (½in) less than desired length.

Dec Round 1: *k2tog, k3, k2tog, k4; rep from * to end of rnd (18 sts).
Next Round: knit.
Dec Round 2: *k2tog, k2; rep from * to end of rnd (12 sts).
Next Round: knit.
Dec Round 3: *k2tog; rep from * to end of rnd (6 sts).

Break yarn. Thread tail through rem sts and fasten off.

FINGERLESS VERSION

Follow glove instructions until hand is complete, ending with round 36 of chart.

For each finger, work as for glove instructions through the end of the set-up round, then work short fingers as follows:

Knit 3 rnds.

Rib Round: *k1, p1; rep from * to end of rnd. Repeat rib round three more times. Cast (bind) off in rib pattern.

FINISHING

Repeat pattern for second glove/fingerless glove.

Weave in ends to WS. Wet-block and shape to size (either flat or on glove blockers) and leave to dry.

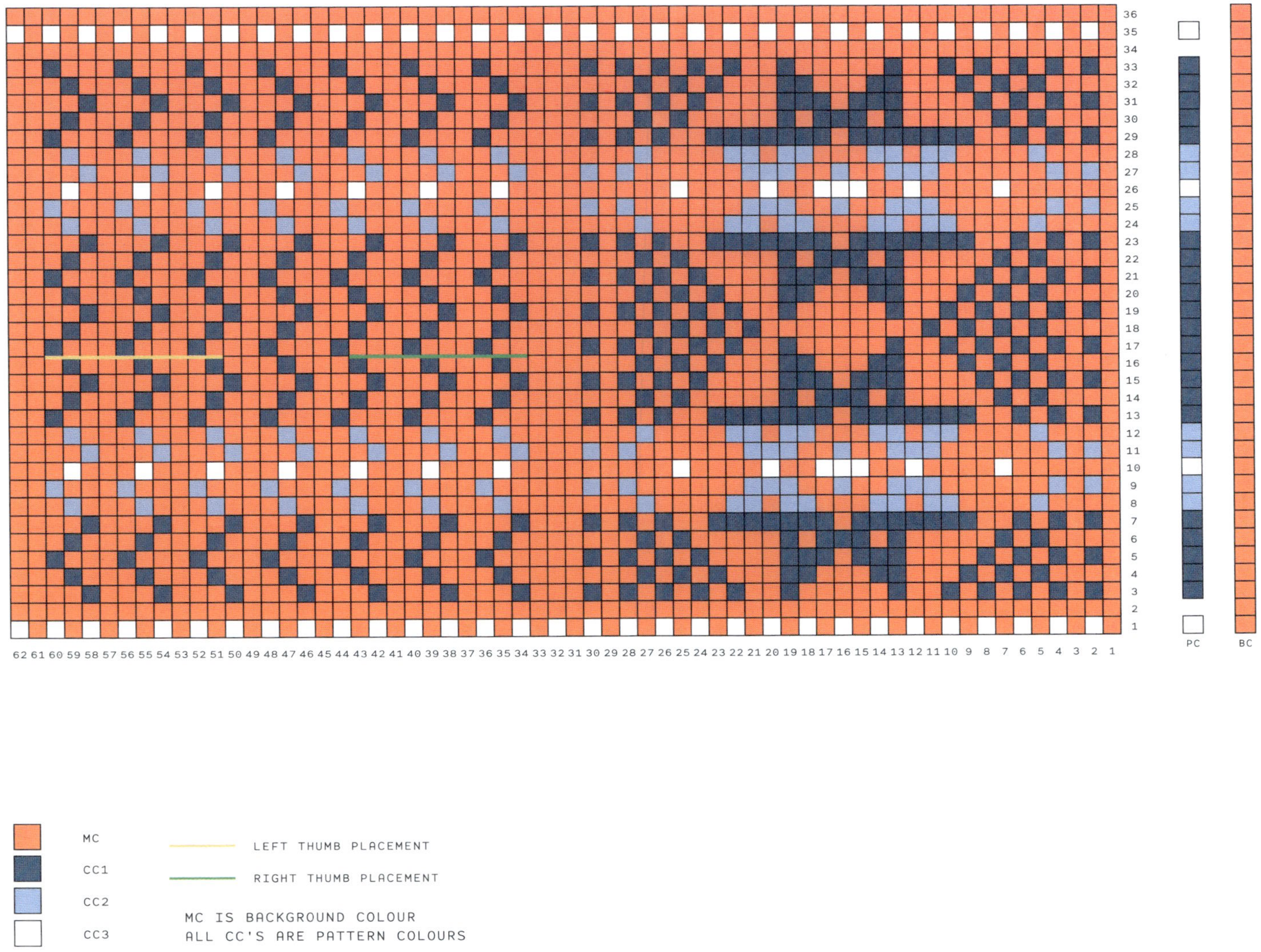
PC
BC
MC
CC1
CC2
CC3
LEFT THUMB PLACEMENT
RIGHT THUMB PLACEMENT
MC IS BACKGROUND COLOUR
ALL CC'S ARE PATTERN COLOURS

PASSING
PLACE

HERITAGE YOKE

by Gudrun Johnston

The inspiration for this piece came from a sweater that my mum designed in the 1970s when she ran The Shetland Trader. I only ever saw photos of it, and her version was an all-over colourwork gansey. For this version, I opted for my favourite sweater style and chose to keep the colourwork just in the yoke. I find the natural earthy tones and classic Fair Isle motifs immediately pleasing to the eye.

CONSTRUCTION

This sweater is worked in one piece from the top down with a circular yoke construction. German Short Rows are used to raise the back neck. After working the charted colourwork yoke, sleeves and body are separated at the underarm, then worked individually down to cuff and hem. Body includes optional A-line waist shaping. The neckline, hem and cuffs are worked in 1×1 rib. Body and sleeve lengths may be adjusted (note that adjustments in length will affect total yarn quantity required of MC).

SIZES

1(2, 3, 4, 5)(6, 7, 8, 9, 10)

FINISHED MEASUREMENTS

Chest circumference: 87.5(93.5, 102.5, 108.5, 114.5)(120.5, 126.5, 134, 141.5, 147.5)cm/34½(36¾, 40¼, 42¾, 45)(47½, 49¾, 52¾, 55¾, 58)in
Hem circumference: 92(98, 107, 113, 119)(125, 131, 138.5, 146, 152)cm/36¼(38½, 42, 44½, 46¾)(49¼, 51½, 54½, 57½, 59¾)in
Front yoke depth: 24(24, 24, 26, 26)(28, 28, 28, 29, 29)cm/9½(9½, 9½, 10¼, 10¼)(11, 11, 11, 11½, 11½)in
Back yoke depth: 26.5(26.5, 26.5, 28.5, 28.5)(30.5, 30.5, 30.5, 32, 32)cm/10½(10½, 10½, 11¼, 11¼)(12, 12, 12, 12½, 12½)in
Side length from underarm: 28(28, 28, 28, 28)(28, 28, 28, 28, 28)cm/11(11, 11, 11, 11)(11, 11, 11, 11, 11)in
Upper sleeve circumference: 30(30.5m 32, 32.5, 34.5)(36, 39, 42, 42, 43.5)cm/11¾(12, 12½, 12¾, 13½)(14¼, 15½, 16½, 16½, 17¼)in
Sleeve length from underarm: 44.5(44.5, 44.5, 44.5, 44.5)(44.5, 44.5, 44.5, 44.5, 44.5)cm/17½(17½, 17½, 17½, 17½)(17½, 17½, 17½, 17½, 17½)in
Neck circumference: 45(45, 47.5, 47.5, 49.5)(49.5, 52, 52, 54, 54)cm/17¾(17¾, 18¾, 18¾, 19½)(19½, 20½, 20½, 21¼, 21¼)in

Designed to be worn with approx. 5–10cm (2–4in) of positive ease. Model is wearing size 3 with approx. 7.5cm (3in) of positive ease.

MATERIALS

Yarn: 4-ply (light fingering) weight yarn in the following approx. amounts:
MC: 795(845, 930, 990, 1040)(1100, 1150, 1220, 1285, 1340)m/870(925, 1015, 1080, 1135)(1200, 1255, 1330, 1405, 1465)yds
CC1: 50(55, 60, 65, 70)(75, 75, 80, 85, 90)m/55(60, 65, 70, 75)(80, 80, 85, 90, 95)yds
CC2: 65(65, 75, 80, 85)(90, 95, 100, 105, 110)m/70(75, 80, 85, 90)(95, 100, 105, 110, 115)yds
CC3: 90(95, 100, 110, 115)(120, 125, 135, 145, 150)m/95(100, 110, 120, 125)(130, 135, 145, 155, 160)yds
CC4: 15(15, 15, 20, 20)(20, 20, 20, 25, 25)m/15(15, 15, 20, 20)(20, 20, 20, 25, 25)yds

Shown in: Jamieson & Smith Heritage (100% Real Shetland Wool, 25g/1oz/110m/120yds) in shades Black (MC), Berry Wine (CC1), Fawn (CC2), Light Grey (CC3) and White (CC4)
MC: 8(8, 9, 9, 10)(10, 11, 12, 12, 13) balls
CC1, CC2 and CC4: 1 ball each
CC3: 1(1, 1, 1, 2)(2, 2, 2, 2, 2) balls

Needles:
Smaller (for Stocking (Stockinette) Stitch and Ribbing): 3.25mm (UK 10, US 3) circular needle, 40cm (16in) length and 80cm (32in) or 100cm (40in) length as well as 3.25mm (UK 10, US 3) set of DPNs*
Larger (for Colourwork): 3.5mm (UK 10/9, US 4) circular needle, 60cm (24in) length and 80cm (32in) or 100cm (40in) length
**For small circumference in the round; alternatively, use a long circular with the Magic Loop method.*

Notions: stitch markers (3 total, 1 distinct for BOR), waste yarn or stitch holders, tapestry needle

TENSION/GAUGE
27 sts and 34 rounds = 10cm (4in) over Fair Isle Pattern worked in the round using larger needle, after blocking

27 sts and 36 rounds = 10cm (4in) over Stocking (Stockinette) Stitch worked in the round using smaller needle, after blocking

PATTERN NOTES

The German Short Row method is used to shape the back neck.

See pattern for how to lengthen body and/or sleeves (additional quantities in MC required).

See Techniques for additional instructions on the following: German Twisted Cast-On, Long-Tail Cast-On, German Short Rows, Backwards Loop Cast-On.

INSTRUCTIONS

YOKE

Using smaller circular needle and MC, CO 120(120, 126, 126, 132)(132, 138, 138, 144, 144) sts as follows (alternatively, use only the Long-Tail Cast-On): Make a slip knot and place it on needle as the first st, CO 1 st using the German Twisted Cast-On, *CO 1 st using the Long-Tail Cast-On, CO 1 st using the German Twisted Cast-On; rep from * until all sts are cast on.

PM for BOR at centre back and join for working in the round, being careful not to twist.

Rib Round: *k1, p1; rep from * to end of rnd.
Work rib round a total of six times or until ribbing measures 2cm (¾in) from cast-on edge.

Next Round: knit.

Work the following increase round according to your size:
Size 1
Inc Round: *(k4, M1L) three times, k3, M1L; rep from * to end of rnd.

Sizes 2–10
Inc Round: *k3, M1L; rep from * to end of rnd.

All Sizes
(32(40, 42, 42, 44)(44, 46, 46, 48, 48) sts inc; 152(160, 168, 168, 176)(176, 184, 184, 192, 192) sts)

Next Round: knit.

Shape Back Neck with German Short Rows
Short Row 1 (RS): k36(38, 40, 40, 42)(42, 44, 44, 48, 48), turn.
Short Row 2 (WS): DS, purl to BOR marker, SM, p36(38, 40, 40, 42)(42, 44, 44, 48, 48), turn

Short Row 3: DS, knit to BOR marker, SM, knit to previous DS, resolve DS, k6, turn.
Short Row 4: DS, purl to BOR marker, SM, purl to previous DS, resolve DS, p6, turn;
Repeat short rows 3 and 4 two more times.

Next round (RS): DS, knit to BOR marker, SM, knit to the first DS encountered, resolve DS by working k2tog, knit until 1 st before the final DS, resolve final DS as follows (technique attributed to Patty Lyons): sl1 kwise, knit the first leg of the DS tbl then psso, knit the second leg of the DS tbl, knit to end of rnd.

Colourwork
Note: change to larger circular needle; change to longer circular needle (same size) during the yoke as needed.

Next Round: work round 1 of Fair Isle Chart to end of rnd.
Last rnd sets chart pattern. Continue to work from chart until round 69 is complete, making increases as shown on the chart.
(190(200, 210, 210, 220)(220, 230, 230, 240, 240) sts inc; 342(360, 378, 378, 396)(396, 414, 414, 432, 432) sts)

Break CC1, CC2, CC3 and CC4.

Change to smaller, longer circular needle.

With MC, knit 1 rnd.

Sizes 1–3
Proceed to All Sizes.

Sizes 4, 5, 6 and 9
Inc Round: *k–(–, –, 21, 22)(11, –, –, 9, –), M1L; rep from * to end of rnd.

Size 7
Inc Round: *k11, M1L, k12, M1L; rep from * to end of rnd.

Size 8
Inc Round: *(k8, M1L) twice, k7, M1L; rep from * to end of rnd.

Size 10
Inc Round: *(k7, M1L) three times, k6, M1L; rep from * to end of rnd.

All Sizes
(0(0, 0, 18, 18)(32, 36, 54, 48, 64) st(s) inc; 342(360, 378, 396, 414)(432, 450, 468, 480, 496) sts)

With MC, knit 3(3, 3, 7, 7)(14, 14, 14, 19, 19) rnds.

Divide for Body and Sleeves
Note: use the Backwards Loop Cast-On when casting on sts in the next rnd.

Division Round: k52(56, 60, 64, 67)(70, 72, 75, 79, 82) for half of back, place next 67(68, 69, 70, 73)(76, 81, 84, 82, 84) sts on waste yarn for right sleeve, CO 6(6, 8, 8, 9)(10, 12, 14, 15, 16) sts for right underarm, PM for side seam, CO another 6(6, 8, 8, 9)(10, 12, 14, 15, 16) sts for right underarm, k104(112, 120, 128, 134)(140, 144, 150, 158, 164) sts for front, place next 67(68, 69, 70, 73)(76, 81, 84, 82, 84) sts on waste yarn for left sleeve, CO 6(6, 8, 8, 9)(10, 12, 14, 15, 16) sts for left underarm, PM for side marker, CO another 6(6, 8, 8, 9)(10, 12, 14, 15, 16) sts for left underarm, k52(56, 60, 64, 67)(70, 72, 75, 79, 82) rem sts for back (232(248, 272, 288, 304)(320, 336, 356, 376, 392) sts rem for body).

BOR marker remains at centre back.

BODY

Work in st st without shaping until body measures 7cm (2¾in) from underarm or to desired length before beginning optional waist shaping.

Begin waist shaping (optional: if omitting waist shaping, proceed to 'Work in st st without shaping until body measures' and remove side seam markers on the next rnd worked):
Inc Round: *knit to 2 sts before side seam marker, M1R, k2, SM, k2, M1L; rep from * one more time, knit to end of rnd (4 sts inc).
Repeat Inc round every eighteenth rnd two more times (244(260, 284, 300, 316)(332, 348, 368, 388, 404) sts).

Note: side seam markers can be removed once body increases are finished.

Work in st st without shaping until body measures 23.5cm (9¼in) from underarm or until 4.5cm (1¾in) short of desired length (for hem ribbing).

Rib Round: *k1, p1; rep from * to end of rnd. Work rib round a total of 16 times or until ribbing measures 4.5cm (1¾in).

Cast (bind) off all sts in rib pattern.

SLEEVES

Using smaller needle (DPNs or long circular if using Magic Loop), MC, and starting at centre of underarm, p&k 6(6, 8, 8, 9)(10, 12, 14, 15, 16) underarm sts, knit across 67(68, 69, 70, 73)(76, 81, 84, 82, 84) held sleeve sts, p&k rem 6(6, 8, 8, 9)(10, 12, 14, 15, 16) underarm sts, PM for BOR (79(80, 85, 86, 91)(96, 105, 112, 112, 116) sts).

Knit 9 rnds or until sleeve measures 2.5cm (1in) from underarm.

Dec Round: k1, k2tog, knit to last 3 sts, ssk (modified), k1 (2 sts dec).

Continue working in st st and repeat Dec Round every 10th(10th, 9th, 9th, 8th)(7th, 6th, 5th, 5th, 5th) rnd 11(11, 13, 13, 15)(17, 21, 23, 23, 21) more times (55(56, 57, 58, 59)(60, 61, 64, 64, 72) sts rem).

Work in st st without shaping until sleeve measures 40.5cm (16in) from underarm or until 4cm (1½in) short of desired length (for cuff ribbing).

Sizes 2, 4, 6, 8, 9 and 10
Proceed to All Sizes.

Sizes 1, 3, 5 and 7
Dec Round: k1, k2tog, knit to end of rnd (1 st dec; 54(–, 56, –, 58)(–, 60, –, –, –) sts rem).

All Sizes
Rib Round: *k1, p1; rep from * to end of rnd. Work rib round a total of 14 times or until ribbing measures 4cm (1½in).

Cast (bind) off all sts in rib pattern.

Repeat for second sleeve.

FINISHING

Weave in ends and close any holes at underarms. Soak sweater in cool water and a gentle wool wash (optional) for at least 20 minutes. Remove excess water from fabric by carefully squeezing (not wringing) and then press between towels. Block to finished measurements.

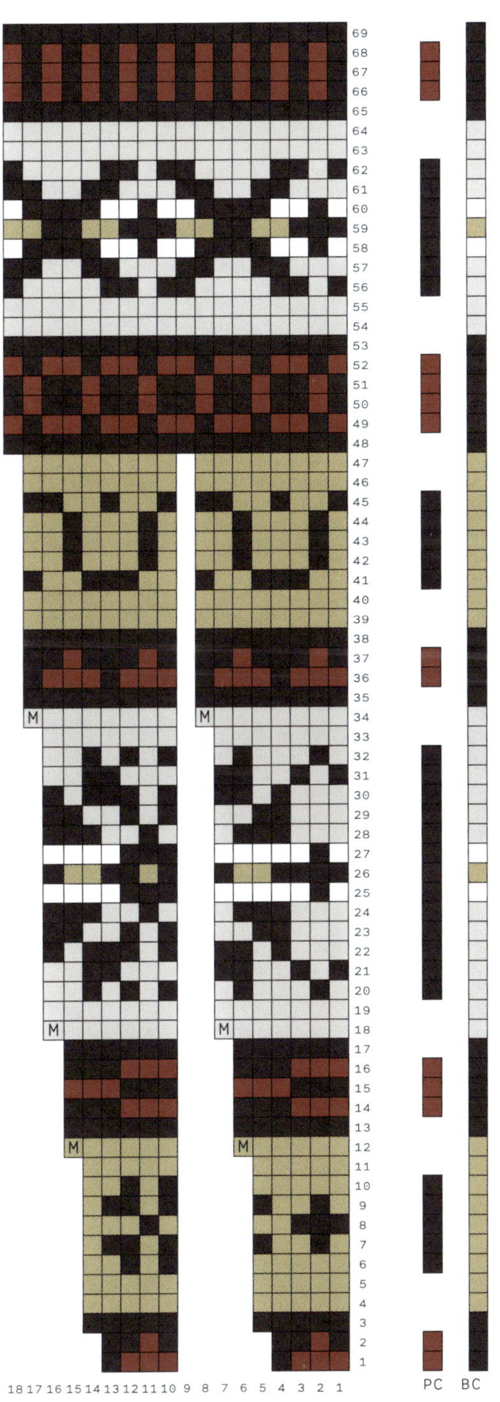
PC
BC

CC4
CC3
CC2
CC1
MC
M M1L
PC PATTERN COLOUR
BC BACKGROUND COLOUR

DOWNSTAIRS SOCKS

by Mary Jane Mucklestone

I run around a lot, racing up and down the steep, narrow stairs of the cottage. Vintage pattern motifs are my obsession, and this arrangement is a favourite. Vertical panels alternate between a small, sweet OXO pattern and zigzags that mimic the stairs I mustn't dash up! How do I hold my yarns when the background and pattern colours switch places within each round? I make a call. I keep the light to the right because it rhymes, so it's easy to remember!

CONSTRUCTION

Worked from the cuff down with a turned heel. Heel stitches are picked up for the gusset and decreased every other round. Heel turn and toe are worked in salt and pepper pattern. The toe is grafted together. Sizing is accomplished by adjusting tension/gauge.

SIZES

1(2, 3)

FINISHED MEASUREMENTS

Finished foot circumference: 20.5(23, 26)cm/ 8(9, 10¼)in
Finished leg length (adjustable): 16(18, 20)cm/ 6½(7, 7¾)in
Choose a size that will result in no ease based on the wearer's foot circumference measured at the widest point (around instep and heel). Leg and foot lengths are adjustable. Sample is shown in size 1.

MATERIALS

Yarn: 4-ply (fingering) weight yarn in the following approx. amounts:
MC: 95(120, 145)m/105(130, 160)yds
CC1: 95(120, 145)m/105(130, 160)yds
CC2: 80(90, 115)m/85(100, 125)yds
CC3: 80(90, 115)m/85(100, 125)yds
Note: yarn quantity may vary depending on leg length, foot length, and yarn type used.

Shown in: Jamieson & Smith 2-ply Jumper Weight (100% Shetland Wool; 25g/1oz/115m/125yds) in shades 202 Light Fawn (MC), 9097 Orangey Red (CC1), 121 Marled Yellow (CC2), and 135 Medium Navy (CC3)
MC: 1(2, 2) ball(s)
CC1: 1(2, 2) ball(s)
CC2: 1(1, 2) ball(s)
CC3: 1(1, 2) ball(s)

Needles:
Needle size varies for different sized socks.
Ribbing: 2(2.25, 2.75)mm/UK 14(13, 12)/US 0(1, 2)
Main: 2.25(2.75, 3.25)mm/UK 13(12, 10)/US 1(2, 3)

Size 1: 2mm (UK 14, US 0) and 2.25m (UK 13, US 1)* set of DPNs
Size 2: 2.25m (UK 13, US 1) and 2.75mm (UK 12, US 2)* set of DPNs
Size 3: 2.75mm (UK 12, US 2) and 3.25mm (UK 10, US 3)* set of DPNs

**For small circumference in the round, alternatively, use a long circular with the Magic Loop method.*

Notions: locking stitch marker or safety pin, tapestry needle

TENSION/GAUGE

Measured over Fair Isle Pattern worked in the round using larger needle after blocking:

Size 1: 36 sts and 36 rounds = 10cm (4in)
Size 2: 32 sts and 32 rounds = 10cm (4in)
Size 3: 28 sts and 28 rounds = 10cm (4in)

PATTERN NOTES

Holding the yarn: because the pattern and background colours change with the two pattern elements, I assign a position for the 'light' coloured yarn and the 'dark' coloured yarn. To make it easy to remember, I usually position the 'light to the right.'

Foot length is easily adjusted by extending the charted pattern in increments of 8 rounds to accommodate either an 'O' or 'X' motif of the Fair Isle pattern. To lengthen the leg, plan ahead and add length before the beginning of the chart so the heel flap and gusset will match the Gusset Chart; each 8-round O or X motif adds 3(2.5, 2)cm/1¼(1, ¾)in. If lengthening, more yarn may be required.

See Techniques for additional instructions on the German Twisted Cast-On and Grafting.

STITCH PATTERNS

Salt and pepper stitch
Row 1 (RS): *k1 with MC, k1 with CC3; rep from * to end of row.
Row 2 (WS): *p1 with CC3, p1 with MC; rep from * to end of row.

INSTRUCTIONS

LEG

Using ribbing needle(s) and MC, CO 72 sts using the German Twisted Cast-On or your favourite stretchy cast-on.

Place locking ring marker for BOR and join for working in the round, being careful not to twist.

Rib Round: *k1, p1; rep from * to end of rnd.
Work rib round until ribbing measures 2.5cm (1in) from cast on edge.

Change to main needle(s) and knit 1 rnd with MC.

Next Round: work across 24 sts of round 1 of Main Chart three times to end of rnd.
Last rnd sets chart pattern. Work rounds 1–48 of chart. Break yarns.

HEEL FLAP

Place first 37 sts of rnd onto a needle or stitch holder to be held for instep. Place last 35 sts of rnd onto another needle for heel flap.

At right edge of heel sts with RS facing (opposite from BOR), join CC1 and CC2.

Working flat (k on RS, p on WS), follow rows 1–20 of Heel Flap Chart (note that 2 sts will be increased on row 1). At the beginning of every row take care to catch the colour not in use. When changing to a new pair of colours, you may carry the unused pair up the right edge of the fabric, trapping them on a RS row with the working yarn. Alternatively, break and knot or weave in ends.

When row 20 is complete, break CC1 and CC2 (37 sts).

HEEL TURN

Note: heel turn is worked flat in Salt and Pepper pattern, alternating MC (light) and CC3 (dark). Work each decrease and its subsequent st in Salt and Pepper pattern as given below. Sometimes the last st will be the same colour, but no worries; it won't be noticeable on the finished sock.

If yarns were not carried up the side of the heel flap, rejoin MC and CC3 at right edge of heel flap with RS facing.

Set-up Row (RS): *k1 with MC, k1 with CC3; rep from * to last st, k1 with MC, turn.
Row 1 (WS): p22 in Salt and Pepper pattern, p2tog, p1, turn (36 sts rem).
Row 2 (RS): k9 in Salt and Pepper pattern, k2tog tbl, k1, turn (35 sts rem).

Row 3: purl in Salt and Pepper pattern to 1 st before gap, p2tog, p1, turn (1 st dec).
Row 4: knit in Salt and Pepper pattern to 1 st before gap, k2tog tbl, k1 turn (1 st dec).
Repeat rows 3 and 4, always working together the 2 sts on each side of the gap, until 23 sts rem, ending on a RS row.

Break yarns.

GUSSET

With RS facing, rejoin CC1 and CC2 at right edge of heel flap where it meets the instep (opposite corner from BOR). In the next round, you will work the Salt and Pepper pattern, alternating CC1 and CC2.

Set-up Round: beginning with CC2, and alternating with CC1, p&k 19 sts along left edge of heel flap, k23 heel sts, p&k 19 sts along right edge of heel flap (98 sts total: 61 sts for gusset and heel, 37 held instep sts).

If using DPNs, divide heel and gusset sts onto two needles. Place locking ring marker for BOR, which is now back to its original position.

Round 1: working across instep, work row 1 of Main Chart across 24 sts, then work sts 1–13 from Main Chart one more time, PM, work row 1 of Gusset & Sole Chart to end of rnd (2 sts dec; 96 sts).

Next Round: work next rnd of Main Chart to marker, SM, work next row of Gusset & Sole Chart to end of rnd.

Work in pattern as established until Gusset & Sole Chart is complete (72 sts rem; 37 instep sts and 35 heel sts).

FOOT

Continue working Main Chart across instep sts and resume working Main Chart across sole sts (beginning with round 26) until round 48 of Main Chart is complete or until approx. 5(6.5, 7.5)cm/ 2(2½, 3) short of desired foot length, finishing at the halfway point or end of an 'O' or 'X' motif if possible. Break MC and CC3.

TOE

Note: the toe is worked in Salt and Pepper pattern with CC1 and CC2.

Arrange sts with 36 instep sts on one needle and 36 sole sts divided across 2 needles if using DPNs or 36 sts on each needle for Magic Loop.

Set-up Round: *k1 with CC1, k1 with CC2; rep from * to end of rnd.

Dec Round 1: ssk with CC1, *k1 with CC2, k1 with CC1; rep from * to last 2 sts before end of instep, k2tog with CC2, ssk with CC1, *k1 with CC2, k1 with CC1; rep from * to last 2 sts before end of sole, k2tog with CC2 (4 sts dec).
Round 2: *k1 with CC2, k1 with CC1; rep from * to end of rnd.
Dec Round 3: ssk with CC2, *k1 with CC1, k1 with CC2; rep from * to last 2 sts before end of instep, k2tog with CC1, ssk with CC2, *k1 with CC1, k1 with CC2; rep from * to last 2 sts before end of sole, k2tog with CC1 (4 sts dec).
Round 4: *k1 with CC1, k1 with CC2; rep from * to end of rnd.
Work rounds 1–4 a total of six times (24 sts rem).

Graft the two sets of 12 sts together to close the toe using either colour of yarn per your preference.

FINISHING

Weave in all ends. Wet-block to size.

Repeat pattern for second sock.

MAIN CHART

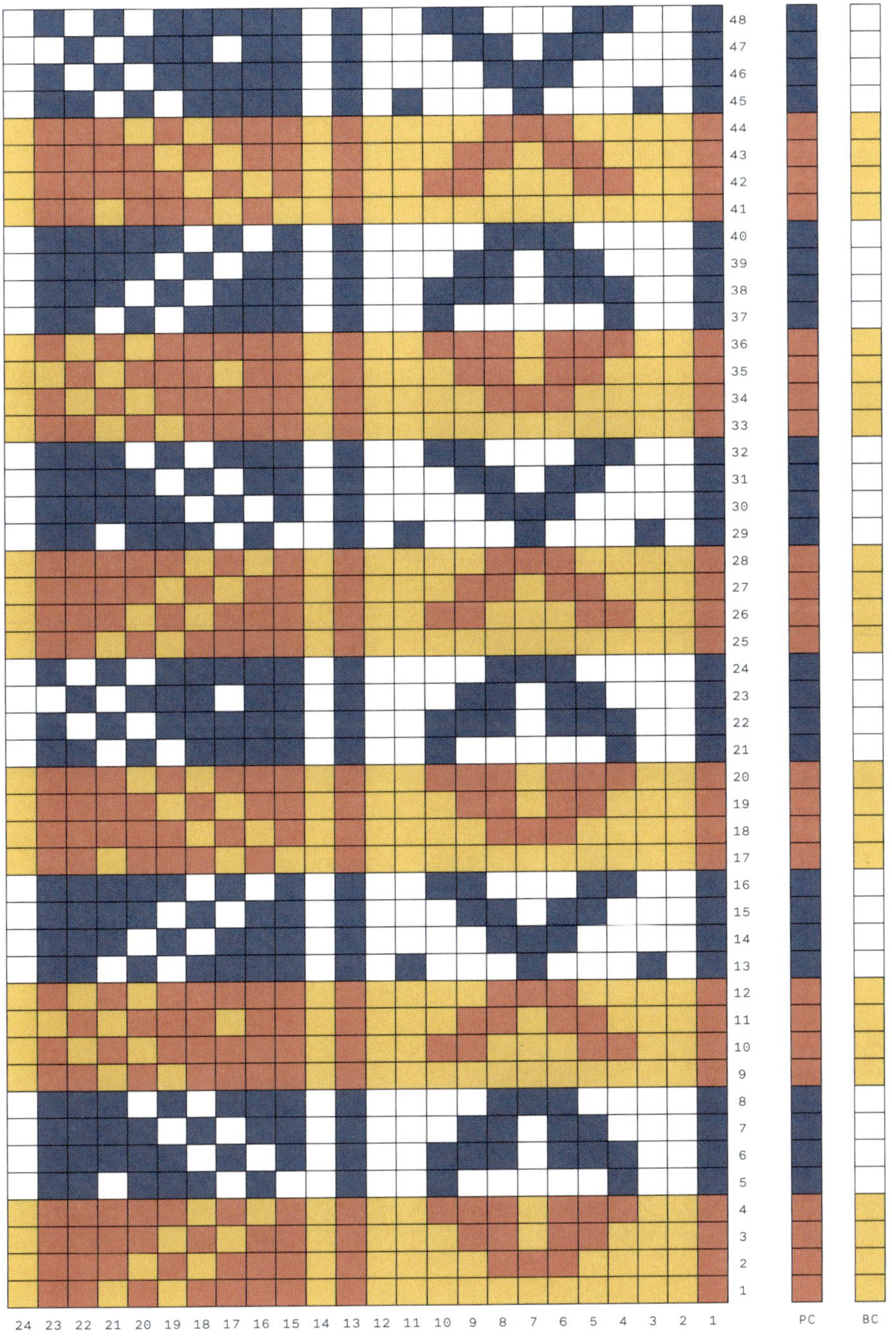

(white)	MC
(orange-brown)	CC1
(yellow)	CC2
(navy)	CC3
PC	PATTERN COLOUR
BC	BACKGROUND COLOUR

HEEL FLAP CHART

GUSSET & SOLE CHART

VIRDEK SHAWL

by Gudrun Johnston

A virdek is a pile of stones acting as some type of marker. The interlocking and defined texture in this shawl evokes a carefully stacked cairn where one might look wistfully out to sea wrapped in Shetland wool. The construction gives a nod to the modern method of knitting traditional Shetland haps, where pleasing little yarn-over loops are made to facilitate the shaping – and in this case, form a simple decorative edge.

CONSTRUCTION

This shawl features a geometric textured pattern worked sideways in two pieces, which are then joined with a Three-Needle Cast- (Bind-) Off for an exposed seam. The texture pattern can be worked from charts or written instructions.

SIZE

One size

FINISHED MEASUREMENTS

Width: 175cm (68¾in)
Depth: 68cm (26¾in)

MATERIALS

Yarn: Approx. 735cm (800yds) of 4-ply (fingering) weight yarn

Shown in: Jamieson's of Shetland Spindrift (100% pure Shetland wool; 25g/1oz/105m/115yds) in shade 230 Yellow Ochre
8 balls

Needles:
Main: 4mm (UK 8, US 6) circular needle, 80cm (32in) length
Finishing (for Three-Needle Cast- (Bind-) Off):
1 spare circular main needle, 80cm (32in) length and 1 needle one size smaller than main needle

Notions: waste yarn, tapestry needle, stitch markers (optional, for separating out the lace repeats; see Pattern Notes), blocking wires (optional)

TENSION/GAUGE

21 sts and 32 rows = 10cm (4in) over Textured Pattern worked flat using main needle, after blocking

PATTERN NOTES

Yarn overs are made along one side (at the beginning of WS rows for the Right Triangle and at the beginning of RS rows for the Left Triangle) to shape each triangular piece. See Techniques for how to work a yarn over at the beginning of a row.

Also see Techniques for additional instructions on the Three-Needle Cast- (Bind-) Off.

The stitch pattern may be worked from either charted or written instructions. *Note that the pattern repeats shift in the written instructions.* The written instructions can be found on our Bookmarked Hub – www. bookmarkedhub.com

INSTRUCTIONS

RIGHT TRIANGLE

Using main circular needle, make a slip knot and place on needle as the first st.
Kfb into the slip knot (2 sts).

Begin working from Chart A starting with the Set-up Row (a WS row).
Work through row 58 (32 sts).

Next work rows 1–24 of Chart B one time (if working directly from the chart, there will not be any repeated sections when working through this chart the first time) (12 sts inc; 44 sts).

Repeat rows 1–24 of Chart B eight more times (96 sts inc; 140 sts).
Note: each repeat of rows 1–24 will add 12 sts.

Break yarn, leaving a long tail for a Three-Needle Cast- (Bind-) Off.

Place all live sts onto a piece of waste yarn.

LEFT TRIANGLE

Using main circular needle, make a slip knot and place on needle as the first st.
Kfb into the slip knot (2 sts).

Begin working from Chart C starting with row 1 (RS).
Work through row 58 (31 sts, 1 fewer st than for the Right Triangle).

Next work rows 1–24 of Chart D one time (if working directly from the chart, there will not be any repeated sections when working through this chart the first time) (12 sts inc; 43 sts, 1 fewer st than for Right Triangle).
Repeat rows 1–24 of Chart D eight more times (96 sts inc; 139 sts).
Note: each repeat of rows 1–24 will add 12 sts.

Note: the next row will add 1 st, bringing the Left Triangle st count to equal that for the Right Triangle.

Knit one more RS row working the same first 5 stitches as row 23 of Chart D up to the second YO and knitting all other stitches (140 sts).

Break yarn leaving a short tail for weaving in. Leave live sts on needle.

With both sets of sts on two separate main needles, work a Three-Needle Cast- (Bind-) Off with a needle one size smaller and with WS held together for an exposed seam.

FINISHING

Weave in ends.

Soak shawl in cold or tepid water using a gentle wool wash (optional) for at least 20 minutes. Remove excess water from fabric by carefully squeezing (not wringing) and then gently roll shawl up in a towel. Block to finished measurements.

For best results, block shawl using blocking wires. First, thread a wire through the yarn over loops along the two sides of the triangle. For the top edge you can either block it straight or catch the edge's slight undulations to emphasize those.

CHART A

58
57
56
55
54
53
52
51
50
49
48
47
46
45
44
43
42
41
40
39
38
37
36
35
34
33
32
31
30
29
28
27
26
25
24
23
22
21
20
19
18
17
16
15
14
13
12
11
10
9
8
7
6
5
4
3
2
1
SET-UP ROW

CHART B

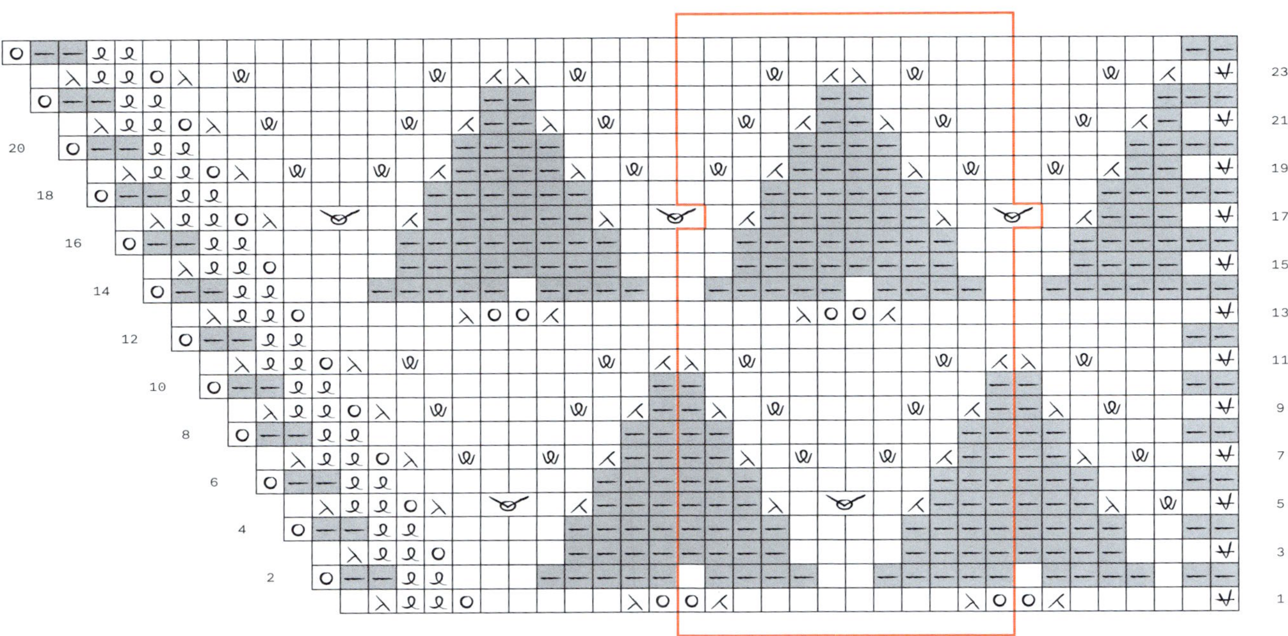

- REPEAT
- KNIT ON RS, PURL ON WS
- PURL ON RS, KNIT ON WS
- SLIP 1 PURLWISE WITH YARN IN FRONT
- K2TOG
- SSK (MODIFIED)
- YO - NOTE THAT SOMETIMES TWO YARN OVERS ARE MADE BACK TO BACK
- K1TBL ON RS ROWS P1TBL ON WS ROWS
- M1L
- M2

CHART C

CHART D

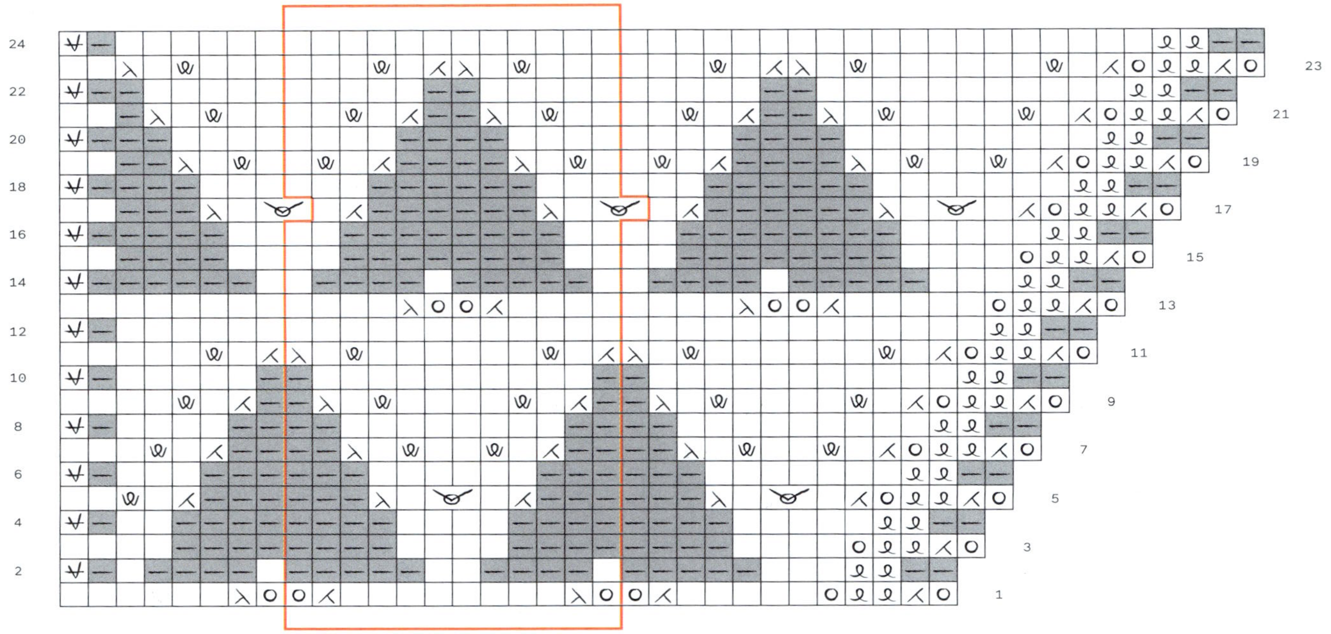

- REPEAT
- KNIT ON RS, PURL ON WS
- PURL ON RS, KNIT ON WS
- SLIP 1 PURLWISE WITH YARN IN FRONT
- K2TOG
- SSK (MODIFIED)
- YO - NOTE THAT SOMETIMES TWO YARN OVERS ARE MADE BACK TO BACK
- K1TBL ON RS ROWS P1TBL ON WS ROWS
- M1L
- M2

FREE DAY IN TOWN

by Mary Jane Mucklestone

Don't let the small size and population fool you; Lerwick is no sleepy backwater. Home to a third of Shetland's population, it boasts excellent museums, a world-class performing arts centre, and dozens of locally owned shops that larger towns can only dream of. The compact size means that it's easy to get around.

Parking on Victoria Pier at the harbour places us in the centre of Lerwick's old town. Originally developed during the Dutch herring trade in the seventeenth century, the town grew organically without formal planning. As a result, the buildings are jumbled tightly together and often sit at odd angles, adding to the picturesque and eclectic character of the area.

Our group is set free at Market Cross, an open square at the centre of Commercial Street known locally as 'Da Street', and the heart of the district. This mostly-pedestrian flagstone street is gaily decorated with fluttering pennants, meandering from Fort Charlotte in the north to the Lodberries In the south, tracing the original shoreline. Despite being only a six-minute walk from end to end, the variety of independent shops and restaurants makes it easy to spend hours exploring. We offer suggestions, but our knitters love discovering the town on their own.

Some folks make a beeline for Jamieson's of Shetland's wool shop, while others seek out the Shetland Times Bookshop for an excellent selection of Shetland-related books, including knitting books.

A favourite stop is The Peerie Shop, directly on the harbour. Small, as the name implies, but loaded to the rafters with captivating goods curated with panache. Unusual Shetland souvenirs, contemporary jewellery and amusing trinkets make it hard to leave empty-handed. It's the only place to find Victoria Gibson's modern knitwear. Decades before the current trend in marled yarns and shifting colour, Gibson was blending colours of Shetland wool and making textured gansey-style knits.

We always encourage wandering the lanes that run perpendicular to Da Street. Some are so narrow you can touch each side with your fingertips, and some so steep they become stairs.

Eventually, we all make our way to the Lodberries; originally private wharves and storehouses partly constructed in the water, with doorways facing the sea, providing a convenient way to load and unload boats for trade and smuggling! The oldest, dating from 1772, is famous as the residence of Detective Inspector Jimmy Perez in the TV series *Shetland*, and is a prime group-photo opportunity.

Unexpectedly sandwiched between two lodberries is Bain's Beach. We love to laze on the sand and search for sea glass and pottery fragments, the crystal-clear water tempting us to take a dip. Occasionally, Dim Riv, a replica Viking longboat, sails by, making a magical time-warp moment.

A little further afield at historic Hay's Dock, the Shetland Museum provides a fascinating glimpse into Shetland's distinctive way of life and past. Exhibits feature geology, prehistoric settlements, Viking heritage, and maritime and crofting customs. My favourites are the elegant stone knives and a large clump of butter found in a bog, and churned around AD 1030. I like to pass through the exhilarating four-storey Boat Hall and up the stairs to view the nationally recognized textile collection, showcasing the weaving, spinning, Fair Isle knitting and fine lacework for which Shetland is famous.

The museum's display of the Gunnister Man is a must-see for wool enthusiasts. Dating back to c.a. 1700, he was found in a bog with his clothing intact. Textile Collection curator Dr Carol Christiansen and a team of experts recreated his outfit, which features two knit caps, long stockings, fancy knitted gloves, and a pouch believed to be the earliest example of two-colour knitting in Shetland.

A knitter's visit to Lerwick would not be complete without seeing the Shetland Textile Museum and Jamieson & Smith (J&S); as they're both on the way out of town, we reunite as a group for our visits.

Jamieson & Smith Wool Brokers sources wool from over 700 local crofters and farmers for producing wonderful yarns, knitwear, blankets, carpets, and other goods. Our special treat is meeting Oliver Henry, who, now retired, worked for the company for over 50 years and is the most charismatic ambassador for Shetland wool.

We gather in the wool shed, where bales and baskets of wool in every natural shade are stacked high up to the ceilings. A natural storyteller, Oliver shares with us his rich knowledge of Shetland wool, from breed characteristics and industry history, to current economics. He demonstrates wool grading, sorting raw wool based on colour, quality and texture, and discusses each grade's uses, from delicate lace yarn to sturdy rugs; none is wasted.

Moving through to the shop, we browse J&S's extensive line of 100% Shetland wool yarn, from cobweb lace to Aran weight. Of particular interest is their Shetland Heritage line, developed in conjunction with the Shetland Museum to replicate the original characteristics of handspun 'wursit' used in old Fair Isle garments. Our wool-savvy travellers have brought extra bags for just such a 'yarny' opportunity!

Our last stop is The Shetland Textile Museum housed in The Bod of Gremista. The walk is lined by a handknit lace fence and bright Fair Isle jumpers stretched on woolly boards flank the entrance. Once a storehouse for the early fishing trade, it's now the intimate setting for an extensive collection of Shetland textiles and knits. Volunteers often demonstrate expert spinning and knitting and the small museum shop features the work of top Shetland designers.

It's the perfect finale for our trip, exemplifying the links between knitting, commerce, creativity and the seafaring traditions of Shetland. Filled with fresh ideas, we begin to plot and plan for a return visit to the islands.

THANK YOU

We have many people to thank for the contents of this book. Some have had a very practical hand in its creation, and others have had a significant influence on us in a variety of ways that have helped shape this into being.

We can't possibly mention everyone by name but know we appreciate you all!

Thank you to:
All the Grand Shetland Adventurers who joined us on our trips. We are so grateful for your trust in letting us share Shetland with you and getting to see it fresh and new every time through your eyes.

Sini and Jonna for jumping on board with the publication. We knew it would shine through the Laine lens and we couldn't be happier with the outcome and collaboration.

Jessica Schwab and Jen Hurley for their tech editing and supportive cheers throughout the process.

The test knitters, sample knitters and preview knitters. We appreciate your time, skill, and feedback to making these patterns the best they can be.

All our Shetland-based friends – those in the knitwear industry and not! You have always given us the very best Shetland welcome.

Pierre. We will be forever grateful that you agreed to let a band of knitters take over Burrastow House for a week of adventure.

Sorley for expertise on all things Shetland (except knitting), skilful manoeuvering of minibus driving, and expert logistical organization!

Laughton for letting your home be our landing place on arrival to Shetland and for among many other things, fish pie!

Our families for letting us spend so much time in Shetland!

Our fans and supporters worldwide. This book is for you.